D0572767

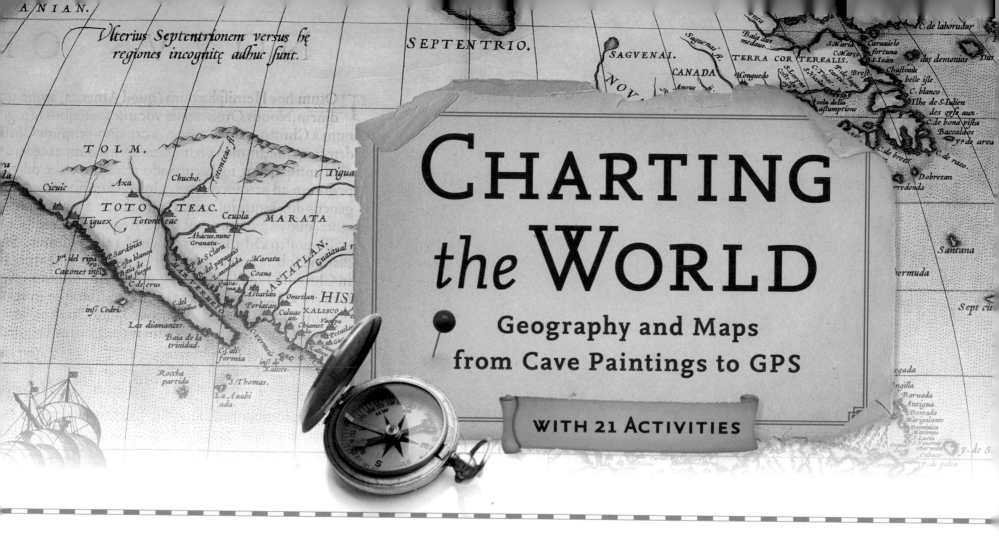

CHARTING the WORLD

Geography and Maps
from Cave Paintings to GPS

WITH 21 ACTIVITIES

RICHARD PANCHYK

Library of Congress Cataloging-in-Publication Data

Panchyk, Richard.

   Charting the world : geography and maps from cave paintings to GPS with 21 activities / Richard Panchyk.

     p. cm.

   Includes bibliographical references and index.

   ISBN 978-1-56976-344-5

   1. Maps—History—Juvenile literature. 2. Cartography—Juvenile literature. 3. Map reading—Juvenile literature. I. Title.

   GA105.6.P36 2011

   912—dc23

                2011019317

Cover and interior design: Monica Baziuk

Activity illustrations: Mark Baziuk

Maps and photos courtesy Library of Congress unless otherwise indicated

Front cover images: Map of the Americas by Abraham Ortelius, 1570, © 2000 Visual Language®; World War II–era compass, © iStockphoto.com/Vikram Raghuvanshi; aerial photograph of a river in Colorado, © iStockphoto.com/Douglas Van Voorst; artist's rendering of a satellite in earth's orbit, Neo Edmund/Shutterstock.com; aerial photograph of Te Wahipounamu, New Zealand, Sam D'Cruz/Shutterstock.com; detail of Columbus Monument, Barcelona, Spain, Alejandro Mendoza R/Shutterstock.com

4913 8463 3/12

Published by Chicago Review Press, Incorporated

814 North Franklin Street

Chicago, Illinois 60610

ISBN 978-1-56976-344-5

Printed in the United States of America

5 4 3 2 1

For Matt and Beth

Contents

Acknowledgments

Thanks to Jerry, Cynthia, and the whole team at Chicago Review Press for their continuing dedication to producing high-quality children's nonfiction. Thanks also to my family and friends for their continued support.

TIME LINE

25,000 years ago	One of the earliest known maps created on a rock in present-day Czech Republic
14,000 years ago	Map drawn on cave wall in present-day Navarra, Spain
4,300 years ago	Babylonians begin using clay tablet maps
9th century B.C.	Greek writer Homer writes *The Odyssey*
4th century B.C	Pytheas sails to Great Britain and maps its coastline
3rd century B.C	Eratosthenes accurately calculates circumference of Earth
2nd century A.D.	Ptolemy publishes "Geography"
1271	Marco Polo leaves for China
1434	Gil Eannes rounds Cape Bojadar, Africa
1454	Printing press invented
1486	Bartholomew Diaz rounds the Cape of Good Hope, Africa
1492	Columbus reaches the New World
1507	Martin Waldseemuller proposes the name "America"
1513	Vasco de Balboa discovers the Pacific Ocean
1544	Sebastian Munster publishes *Cosmographia*

1569 Mercator introduces the Mercator projection

1590s Copper plate method begins to replace woodcuts for mapmaking

1607 Jamestown, Virginia, settled

1675 Royal Observatory founded at Greenwich, England

1720s John Harrison develops marine chronometer to help find longitude at sea

1763 Charles Mason and Jeremiah Dixon hired to survey the Pennsylvania/Maryland border

1784 Survey of the Mason-Dixon Line is completed

1803 Louisiana Purchase greatly expands US territory

1828 First operational railroad

1844 Presidential candidate James K. Polk uses "54-40 or Fight!" in campaign

1848 California Gold Rush causes many settlers to head west

1879 United States Geological Survey (USGS) is created

1883 *Treasure Island* written, popularizing the idea of the treasure map

1884 Greenwich, England, set as location for the prime meridian

1890s First automobiles hit the road

1905 Photolithography is introduced

1914–18 Aerial photography becomes popular

1920s Road maps introduced

1945 Major changes to world map after World War II ends

1940s–50s Modern-day highway system begins to be developed

1972 Landsat 1 is launched

1981 GPS system becomes operational

1990s Major changes to world map with end of Communism and breakup of Soviet Union

INTRODUCTION

MY PASSION for geography and maps goes back to my childhood. Maybe this is because I traveled so much when I was young, and I was exposed to so many new and exciting places.

To me, maps had a magical way of reducing vast and distant lands to manageable sizes, so that I could conquer these places in my imagination and easily follow wide rivers, climb high mountain peaks, and cross great deserts with the tip of my finger. Looking at my colorful maps, I could imagine what life would be like high up in the Andes, or deep in the swamplands of Louisiana, or perhaps in frost-covered Greenland. I treasured my world atlas. On a rainy afternoon, I'd open my US map and color in the most remote places, imagining that I might live there when I grew up. I fancied myself a pioneer, venturing where nobody had gone before, to one of the few blank spots on the map.

I've tried to cover a lot of ground in this book to give you an overview of the many fascinating aspects of geography and maps. My hope is that reading my book will encourage you to further explore the subject.

➣ An 1880s map of Greenland, one of a series of cards given away by the Arbuckle Coffee Company.

GEOGRAPHICALLY SPEAKING

1

MANY THOUSANDS of years ago, a man stood on a hill, looking down upon the scenery spread before him a hundred feet below. At the far right of his view the terrain was littered with large and small boulders, home to many snakes and lizards but also a good shelter during a stampede. Straight ahead was the vast plain of high grass, dotted with only a few trees and stretching all the way to the high mountains in the far distance. And to the left began a thick forest, which in turn led to a wide river that was home to much wildlife. It was all so easy to see from this vantage point, yet once the man descended the hill, he lost all sense of perspective. Once he set foot into the forest, it was hard to keep track of distance and direction.

Once he walked upon the plain, it was difficult to see where he was going. If only he could preserve this image permanently, he thought; if only he could etch the geography that lay below onto something more dependable than his mind.

Thus was born the first map.

What Is Geography?

THE WORD *geography* is of Greek origin. It comes from the Greek words "geo," meaning earth, and "graphy," meaning writing or describing.

Geography is place. When you set foot outside, you are immediately confronted with geography. Look around. Notice the particular features of your neighborhood. You may live in the heart of a great city, surrounded on all sides by huge skyscrapers. Or perhaps you live in a rural area with nothing in sight except fields. No matter where you live, your geographical location undoubtedly has many unique features, both natural and man-made.

The natural features (or *landforms*) of your location—mountains, hills, plains, deserts, canyons, streams, rivers, lakes, oceans, peninsulas, and islands—are its most basic geographical elements. *Topography*, the details of the earth's surface features, is closely connected to where people live and how they live. Location and surface features determine climate, which in turn determines a num-

ber of other things: the number of people who can live there, the type of crops that can be grown, the types of animals that can live there, and natural resources that can be found.

In short, *where* in the world you live affects *how* you live.

So how did the geography of the world come to be? What forces have shaped it?

Pangaea

EACH OF the earth's physical features was formed in a unique way and at a unique time. Some of the earth's features were formed billions of years ago, some were formed only thousands of years ago, and still others were formed recently. Under a seemingly calm surface, the earth is very restless. Much of the change to the earth's topography has been due to movement of its crust, the surface layer. The earth's crust is not solid and continuous. It is broken into a dozen major pieces, called *plates*, that move and shift (called *plate tectonics*). These motions account for much of the geological unrest on earth, including mountain formation, earthquakes, and volcanic eruptions.

The continents as we know them today did not take their current form until fairly recently. One billion years ago, all the land on the earth was massed together in a giant supercontinent. Between 750 and 540 million years ago, it began to split into pieces that drifted apart. But around 470 million years ago, the plates' movements shifted, and some of the land masses began to drift back toward one another. By about 270 million years ago, these land masses collided to create a supercontinent known as *Pangaea* (from Greek, meaning "all earth" or "all lands"). But just 30 million or so years later, around the time when dinosaurs first began to appear, the plates began to shift again, and Pangaea began to separate once more. Over the years, the continents continued to slowly drift apart.

By the time the last of the dinosaurs became extinct, the continents still did not look quite the way they do today. Even now, continental drift is occurring. North America and Africa are still moving away from each other, causing the Atlantic Ocean to expand. Tectonic plates around the world are moving at a rate between one and six inches per year. It may not seem like much, but over time it adds up.

➤ The earth's landforms look very different today than they did at the time of the first dinosaurs, when the continents were squeezed together in one mass we call Pangaea. This view of Africa and Saudi Arabia was taken from *Apollo 17* on December 7, 1972, on the way to the moon. *Courtesy of NASA*

Crash, Rumble, and Crumble: Forces That Shape the Earth's Geography

THE EARTH's moving plates are the force behind the creation of its major mountains. When plates collide, they cause huge masses of rock to be uplifted. The "young" Rocky Mountains were formed between 50 and 100 million years ago, while the "old" Alleghenies along the East Coast were shaped nearly 300 million years ago, uplifted when North America and Africa collided. The Himalayas, the highest mountains in the world, were formed about 55 million years ago when India collided with Asia. They have continued rising, very slowly, since then.

Besides creating mountains, the constant movement of the earth's plates causes other changes, notably earthquakes. Earthquakes occur along *faults*, the boundaries of two different plates. When the plates shift, either rubbing against each other or pulling apart, an earthquake can occur. The northward-moving Pacific Plate and the southward-moving North American Plate meet along California's San Andreas Fault, the location of the powerful 1906 San Francisco earthquake and the 1989 Loma Prieta earthquake.

Volcanoes are formed because of movement of the earth's plates. They are created when lava flows from the *upper mantle* (the molten layer below the crust) to the surface through cracks, often caused by tectonic movement along fault lines. The lava, volcanic ash, and cinder form a cone around the flow. Volcanic eruptions alter the features of the earth, including the height and shape of the volcanoes themselves. When Mount St. Helens erupted in May 1980, it literally blew

➤ Panoramic view of Pikes Peak, part of the "young" Rocky Mountains, taken in 1919.

4

its top, losing 1,300 feet of height. The eruption also turned more than 200 square miles of surrounding forest into a dead zone, with hot lava, ash, and mud destroying all living things in their path.

There are also other factors are at play in the shaping of our world. Weathering has a major long-term impact on the geological features of the earth. For example, geological evidence has shown that the ancient Allegheny mountain peaks, more than 200 million years older than the Rockies, may have originally towered 35,000 feet high. (The highest Rockies are around 14,000 feet tall.) The Allegheny Mountains have weathered over time, however, dramatically reducing their altitudes and creating a plateau effect—they are not the sharp, high peaks of mountain ranges such as the Rockies. The highest point in the Alleghenies is now 6,711 feet above sea level, and there are more than 40 peaks that reach over 6,000 feet in altitude.

Water erosion is another major factor in the creation of the earth's current geographical features. First, rainwater can slowly erode mountains and hills by carrying soil elsewhere. Eventually, the loss of soil can have a big impact. Major rainfall can cause mudslides and the collapse of whole sections of hills.

➤ A *geodimeter* measures the distance between two points. It is used near active volcanoes because they start to deform as they are about to erupt. This is a photograph of a geodimeter station on Smith Creek Butte near Mount St. Helens in April 1980. *Courtesy of USGS*

In addition, when rain reaches the earth's surface, it runs downhill in any direction that it can. The force of the running water will begin to create a slight channel effect, so that rainwater follows that course every time. With each rainfall, the water will cut the channel deeper and deeper until, after hundreds or thousands of years, it becomes deep enough to turn into a stream or river.

By itself, wind can also cause erosion and shifting, especially in open areas with sand (beaches) or dry, loose soil. Wind is also a major force in creating large waves, which can cause severe beach erosion.

Water can alter geography in other ways. During a hurricane or major storm, surging seas can wash away beaches and alter maps. A 1938 hurricane that hit New England submerged a swath of land along the south shore of Long Island, creating the Shinnecock Inlet, which exists to this day.

Glaciation, the growth and movement of glaciers, has been another factor in shaping geography. Over the last three million years, there have been four ice ages, periods when glaciers have advanced southward, covering much of the earth's northern latitudes. When they are stationary, gla-

➤ LEFT: This geological map of New Jersey from 1894 shows the Terminal Moraine across the state, the line of farthest advance of the glaciers during the last ice age.

➤ RIGHT: Lyell Glacier and Maclure Glacier in Yosemite National Park, California, as they were mapped in 1883 by Willard D. Johnson of the US Geological Survey. Since 1883, they have shrunk in size considerably. *Courtesy of USGS*

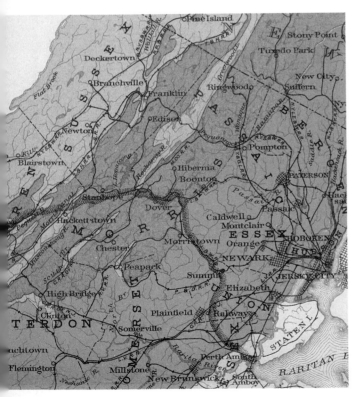

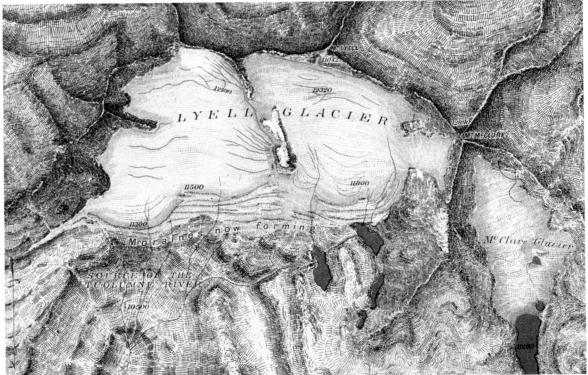

ciers do not cause any change to the earth's features. But their advance and retreat, or forming and melting, can cause major changes. The advance and retreat of glaciers during the last ice age (occurring between about 100,000 years ago and 10,000 years ago) made lasting changes to the Northern Hemisphere's features. They moved boulders, polished rocks, carved valleys, left hill-shaped deposits of glacial soils, and created numerous lakes and ponds. The Great Lakes were formed by glaciers and are the largest glacial lakes in the world. The famous Lake District in England was also formed by glaciers. Only a few small glacier pockets remain in the mountainous parts of the western United States.

Our Changing Understanding of Geography

ALMOST EVERY creature on earth has a sense of geography, of place. Even the smallest animals are aware of their surroundings, and though they cannot describe it in words as we can, they know the difference between a forest and a meadow, a mountain and a valley, or a river and a desert. They know because their lives depend upon it. Whether bird, mammal, or reptile, a creature must know where to go for water, for shelter, for food, to mate, and to raise its young. Each of these activities may

FINDING ELEVATION

DETERMINING the height of hills and mountains is currently done using advanced technology that allows for precise measurement. But there is an easy way to get a fairly accurate measurement of elevation for a small, low hill.

YOU'LL NEED
➤ Yardstick
➤ 50-foot tape measure or ball of twine or string
➤ A friend
➤ Pencil or pen
➤ Notebook
➤ Straight-edge level

Take a field trip to a park or some location with a small, low hill. Start at the base of the hill. Hold the yardstick vertically. Put the end of the tape measure at the top of the yardstick and have your friend extend it toward the slope of the hill. Keep a firm grip on the yardstick to make sure it stays perpendicular to the ground. When the tape measure or string hits the slope of the hill, have your friend mark that spot by sticking a pencil into the ground. Now climb to that position, place the yardstick there, and repeat the process. Each time you do this, you've climbed three feet in elevation—

keep track in a notebook. When you get to the top of the hill, you may need to measure from a lower point on the yardstick, or use a one-foot or six-inch ruler to be more precise.

For a variation on this activity, use your body as the yardstick. Measure the distance from the ground to your eyes. Then hold a straight-edge level in front of your eyes and have your friend climb to a position on the hill so his feet are just on the sight line of the level you are holding. Your friend should mark his spot with a pencil, then have you move to that location, and so forth up the hill.

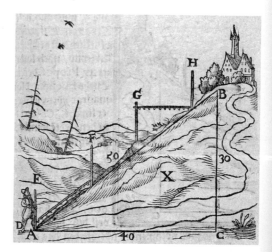

➤ A centuries-old image shows a simple yet reliable method for measuring the height of a hill. *Courtesy of NOAA*

occur in a distinct geographical location within the animal's habitat.

People have always had a keen sense of geography. For as long as humans have been in existence, they have been on the move. In fact, evidence shows that some of our distant ancestors left Africa nearly two million years ago for Asia.

The first humanlike creatures to leave Africa did so 100,000 years ago, and they gradually spread to the rest of the world, reaching North America over the Bering Strait land bridge at least 15,000 years ago. Once they got to the New World, they made their way south and west, populating North America and then South America by 13,000 years ago.

Since humans traveled so widely, their knowledge of geography was essential. Each band of humans had to decide where best to settle. They clearly recognized the different geographical features they saw around them. In addition, they captured what they saw using pictures.

Though humans were probably making maps long before, one of the oldest maps ever discovered is a 25,000-year-old engraving of several local land features, scratched on a rock in the Pavlov region of the Czech Republic. Another ancient map, engraved on a rock in a cave in Navarra, Spain, is believed to be 14,000 years old. A map called the Mezherich map, dating to about 12,000 B.C., has been found in the Ukraine. These early maps are very crude by modern standards, but to the people who made them, they were the best representations of the world they saw around them.

As civilizations grew, so did people's knowledge of geography. Understanding their environment helped them build cities, develop agriculture, and raise livestock. Over time, maps became more sophisticated. The ancient Egyptians, for example, made maps of their roads on wooden tablets and papyrus. The Babylonians also had a detailed geographical understanding of their world and were making maps on clay tablets 4,300 years ago.

The Greeks made great contributions to geographical knowledge. Homer, the ninth-century-B.C. Greek author of the epic poems *The Odyssey* and *The Iliad*, was fascinated by the earth's geography. Homer believed the earth was a flat, circular disk. *The Odyssey* follows a soldier named Odysseus's ten-year journey from Troy to Ithaca. Along the way, Odysseus gets lost and travels to many strange lands and has many adventures.

Anaximander (born around 610 B.C.) was one of the pioneers of *cartography*, or mapmaking. He was believed to have produced a map of the world on a bronze tablet. The map was crude by today's standards but groundbreaking for its time. It showed the known world surrounded by ocean and used the same flat disk idea that Homer did. It was most accurate when showing the lands immediately surrounding the Mediterranean but less precise for lands farther from Greece.

Around the sixth century B.C., with advancements in mathematics and astronomy, ancient Greeks began to accept the idea of the earth as a sphere.

The more the early geographers traveled, the more they were able to detail in maps. The personal knowledge of Herodotus, who lived around 440 B.C., extended to Libya and Ethiopia to the south, India to the east, and Spain to the west. A fourth-century-B.C. Greek explorer named Pytheas sailed to Great Britain and traveled extensively there, further extending the Greeks' knowledge of the world. He even estimated Great Britain's perimeter based on measurements he took along the coast. Pytheas came up with a distance of about 5,000 miles. Though his estimate is far from the true perimeter of Britain (it has over 7,700 miles of coastline, including all the bays and inlets), he was able to provide some idea of the shape of the island.

Eratosthenes (276–194 B.C.) used observations about the sun's position in the sky at both Syrene and Alexandria, as well as the distance between the two places (5,000 stadia), to figure out that distance represented 1/50th of the earth's circumference. He then calculated the circumference to be 250,000 stadia—around 25,000 to 30,000 miles; we are not certain exactly how many stadia make

➤ LEFT: World map according to Strabo (c. 63 B.C.–A.D. 24). He traveled extensively and wrote a book on geography. Like most ancient Greek geographers' maps, his world map was reprinted during the Renaissance.

➤ RIGHT: This 1888 map is a depiction of the world according to the Greek geographer Hecateus (c. 520 B.C.). Hecateus had knowledge of the Nile, Euphrates, Tigris, and Indus Rivers, all the locations of ancient civilizations predating the Greeks, but northern Europe was a vast and unknown place at this time.

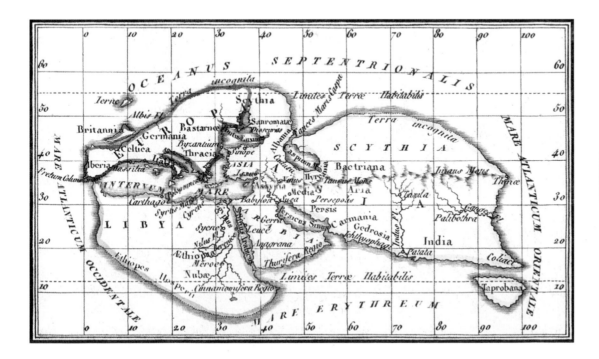

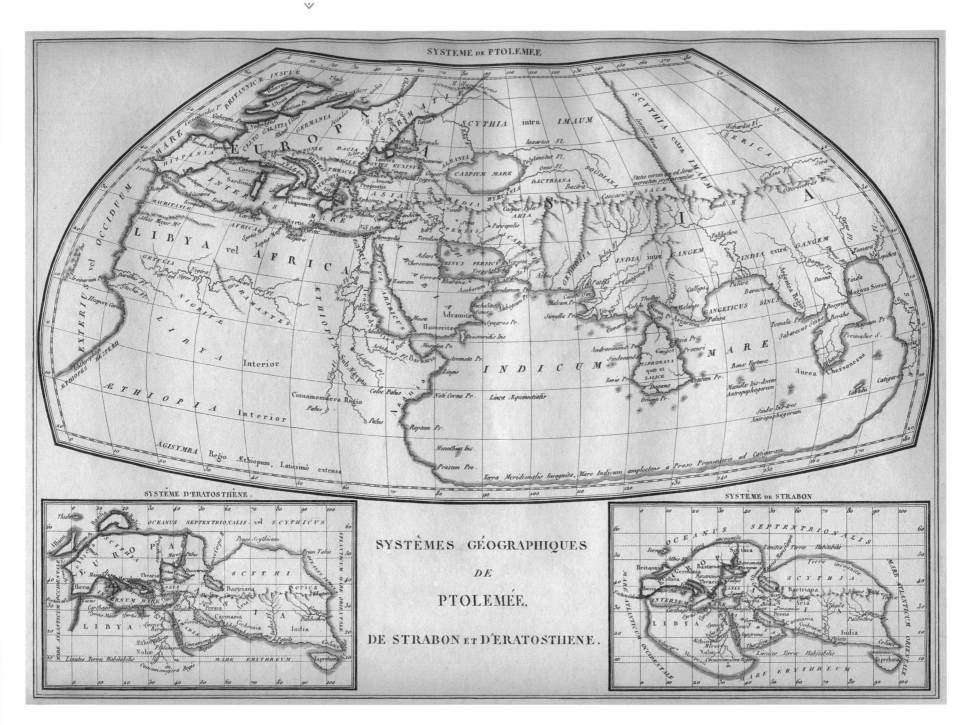

SYSTEME DE PTOLEMEE

SYSTÈME D'ERATOSTHENE.

SYSTÈME DE STRABON

SYSTÈMES GÉOGRAPHIQUES

DE

PTOLEMÉE,

DE STRABON ET D'ERATOSTHENE.

10

up a modern mile—which is very close to the earth's actual circumference of 24,900 miles.

The Roman Empire carried on many of the traditions and scientific advances of the Greeks. Another great contributor to ancient geography and cartography was Ptolemy (c. A.D. 90–165), a Roman citizen living in Egypt. He was the author of a book called *Geography*, in which he described and gave coordinates for numerous places in Europe, Asia, and Africa. His map of the known world was more extensive and more accurate than any that had been done before.

Geography in the Middle Ages

FOLLOWING THE collapse of the Roman Empire in the fifth century A.D., scientific knowledge did not advance very much. The geographical progress that had been made by the Egyptians and Greeks over the centuries slowed. The idea of a spherical earth began to fall out of favor. Instead, people cited passages in the Bible that seemed to contradict the round earth theory.

One of those who pushed the idea of a flat earth was Cosmas Indicopleustes, a sixth-century Egyptian monk. Cosmas wrote a book called *Christian Topography*, which relied heavily on Bible passages to develop a theory of the earth's geography. According to Cosmas, the earth was a flat rectangle that was 400 days' journey in length

and 200 days' journey in width. The land was surrounded on all sides by an ocean. Cosmas wrote in his prologue:

[I] exhort my readers to examine the sketch of the universe and the stellar motions which we have prepared as a representation of the organic sphere of the pagans . . . [and] to overthrow from the foundation the error of the pagan theories.

He continued:

The Deity accordingly having founded the earth, which is oblong, upon its own stability, bound together the extremities of the heaven with the extremities of the earth, making the nether extremities of the heaven rest upon the four extremities of the earth, while on high he formed it into a most lofty vault overspanning the length of the earth. Along the breadth again of the earth he built a wall from the nethermost extremities of the heaven upwards to the summit, and having enclosed the place, made a house, as one might call it, of enormous size, like an oblong vaulted vapour-bath.

What Cosmas pictured was in essence the earth as a canopy bed.

Besides Biblical arguments, Cosmas used logic to try to deflate the idea of a round earth. If people stood on the opposite ends of the supposedly

➤ OPPOSITE: Ptolemy's map was more extensive and more accurate than previous ones. This version was published in 1812.

spherical earth, how could both be standing upright and neither fall off? "When it rains upon both of them, is it possible to say that the rain falls down upon the two, and not that it falls down to the one and falls up to the other, or falls against them, or towards them, or away from them?"

Another person who questioned the idea of a spherical earth was the philosopher St. Augustine (A.D. 354–430), who wrote: "As to the fable that there are ... men on the opposite side of the earth, where the sun rises when it sets on us, men who walk with their feet opposite ours, there is no reason for believing it. Those who affirm it do not claim to possess any actual information; they merely conjecture."

Despite the flat-earth theories that were circulating, there were those who still believed that the earth was round. A learned monk called Venerable Bede (c. A.D. 672–735) was one of those who believed that the earth was indeed spherical. Ultimately, the only thing that would settle the question for good was more exploration of the world.

The Great Age of Exploration

COMMERCE, EXPLORATION, and mapmaking developed hand in hand. As traders sought to expand their range, they looked to maps to help them navigate in new and unfamiliar lands. Marco Polo (1254–1324), the Italian explorer, journeyed from Venice all the way to China beginning in 1271. The geographical knowledge of the Far East that he brought back with him in 1295 helped future mapmakers and explorers. Polo was an excellent observer, and his notes read like a modern-day travel guide, including many geographical details. Here is an extract from his book:

After riding then those ten days from the city of Juju, you find yourself in a kingdom called Taianfu, and the city at which you arrive, which is the capital, is also called Taianfu, a very great and fine city. ... Taianfu is a place of great trade and great industry, for here they manufacture a large quantity of the most necessary equipments for the army of the Emperor. There grow here many excellent vines, supplying great plenty of wine; and in all Cathay this is the only place where wine is produced. It is carried hence all over the country. There is also a great deal of silk here, for the people have great quantities of mulberry trees and silk-worms. From this city of Taianfu you ride westward again for seven days, through fine districts with plenty of towns and boroughs, all enjoying much trade and practicing various kinds of industry. Out of these districts go forth not a few great merchants, who travel to India and other foreign regions, buying and selling and getting gain. After those seven days' journey you arrive at a city called Pianfu, a large and important place, with a number of traders

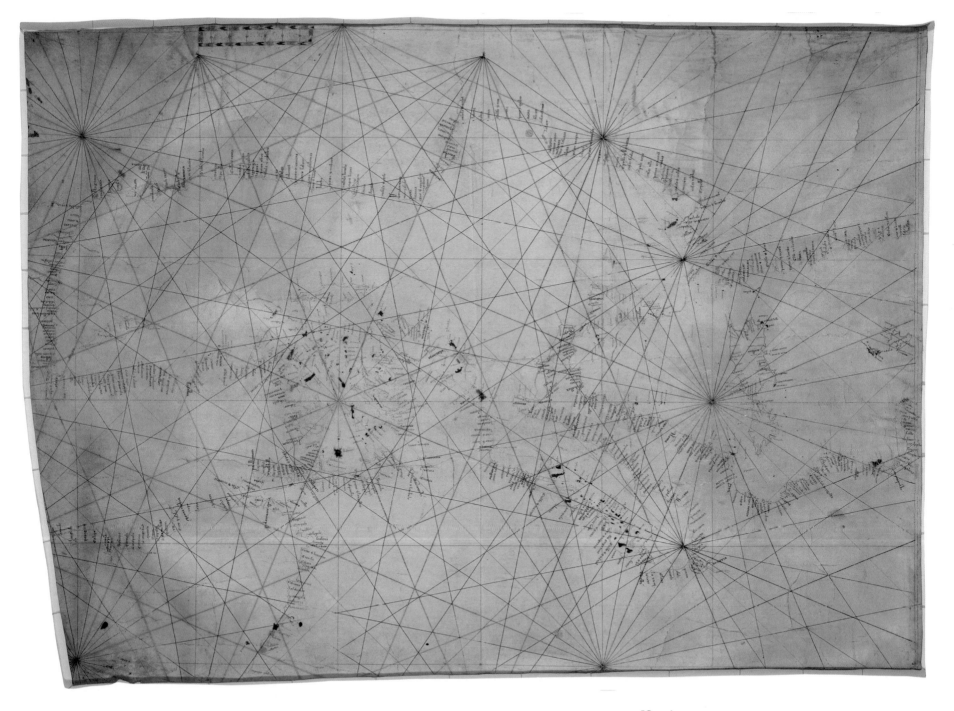

living by commerce and industry. It is a place too where silk is largely produced.

Though Polo's journey was very important, it was nonetheless a land journey to a place that the ancients already knew existed. Extensive voyages by sea were less frequent. Explorers and merchants wanted to find a shortcut to reach the Spice Islands of Asia, but because of extensive and dangerous reefs and turbulent seas, it took until the year 1434 for an explorer named Gil Eannes to round Cape Bojador, Western Sahara, Africa. In 1486, Bartholomew Diaz reached the Cape of Good Hope at the southern tip of Africa.

An Italian astronomer named Toscanelli believed it was possible to reach the Spice Islands by sailing west across the Atlantic Ocean. If correct, it would mean that the earth was spherical, not flat. Toscanelli first detailed this idea in 1474, in a letter and map he sent to the king of Portugal. Around 1480, he sent a copy of the letter and map to Christopher Columbus, who had heard about Toscanelli's theories and asked for more information. It is said that Columbus brought the letter and map with him when he sailed across the Atlantic in 1492. The letter read, in part:

On previous occasion I have spoken to you of a sea route to the land of spice shorter than the one which you take by the way of Guinea. That is the reason why the Most Serene King asks of me . . . an explanation sufficiently clear to enable men . . . to understand the existence of such a route. Although I know that it is a consequence of the spherical form of the earth, I have decided, nevertheless, so as to be better understood and to facilitate the enterprise, to demonstrate in constructing a nautical chart that the said route is proved to exist. I therefore send to His Majesty a map which has been drawn with my own hands, and on which are marked your coasts and the islands which may be taken as a starting point, when you undertake the voyage, by steering constantly towards the west. You will also find thereon the indication of the countries which you must fall in with; how much you will have to deviate from the Pole, and from the [equator]; and finally, the space, that is to say, the number of leagues you have to sail over to reach the country which is so rich in spice and precious stones of all sorts. Do not be surprised if I call the country of spices a western country, whilst it is the custom to call it eastern. The reason is, that in making the voyage by sea in the hemisphere which is opposite our own, that country will always be found on the west side. . . . I have also marked, for the use of navigators, several countries where you may touch, in case contrary winds or some accident should drive mariners to some other coast than the one intended.

Though the Vikings likely preceded him by hundreds of years, Christopher Columbus got credit as the first European to "discover" the New World. On October 12, 1492, the lookout on one of Columbus's ships spotted land, one of the Bahaman islands. Columbus also reached Cuba and Haiti on that voyage, the Lesser Antilles and Jamaica on his second voyage, and Trinidad and mainland South America on his third voyage. In 1502, he made a fourth voyage, landing at Honduras in Central America. The information he gathered greatly expanded European geographical knowledge.

After Columbus's initial voyage, explorers sailed for the Americas by the dozen, seeking fame and fortune. One after another, their discoveries advanced the knowledge of North and South American geography. John Cabot explored in the North Atlantic in 1497; Amerigo Vespucci found the South American coast in 1499; Gaspar

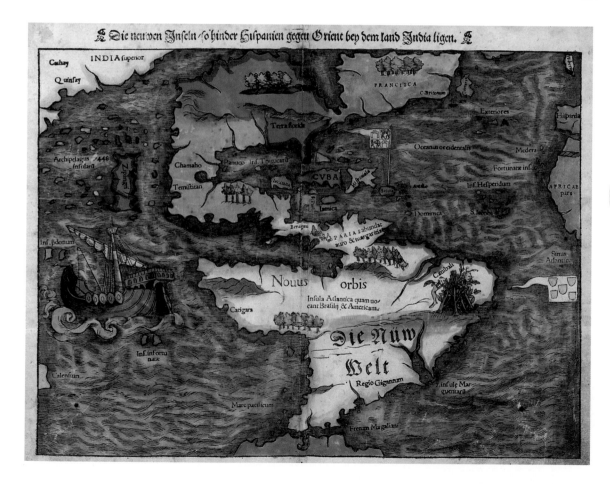

➢ ABOVE: The Atlantic Ocean according to Martin Behaim, 1492.

➢ LEFT: A 1550 map of the New World, by Munster.

Cortoreal explored the North American coast from Labrador to Nova Scotia in 1501; Juan Ponce de Leon discovered Florida in 1512; Vasco de Balboa discovered the Pacific Ocean in 1513; Hernan Cortez (or Cortes) conquered Mexico beginning in 1519; Alonso Alvarez de Pineda discovered the mouth of the Mississippi River in 1519; Giovanni da Verrazzano reached what is now New York Harbor in 1524; Jacques Cartier entered the Gulf of St. Lawrence in Canada in 1534; Francisco Vazquez de Coronado discovered the Grand Canyon in 1539; and Hernando de Soto reached the Mississippi River in 1541. Sir Francis Drake and Sir Thomas Cavendish, both Englishmen, explored the coast of South America and the west coast of North America in the 1570s and 1580s.

Because of rapidly changing information, maps of the New World created during this period vary. Details of both the eastern and western American coastlines, as well as the continent's interior, changed as knowledge of the mysterious land grew. The great age of exploration contributed to an explosion in mapmaking.

The explorers continued to arrive, even as settlements were established all around North America. In 1609, Henry Hudson sailed up the river that now bears his name, and he later explored what is now called the Great Hudson Bay (where he vanished in 1611); Samuel de Champlain explored the Great Lakes in 1609; following his 1613 voyage, Adriaen Block (who named Block Island off the coast of

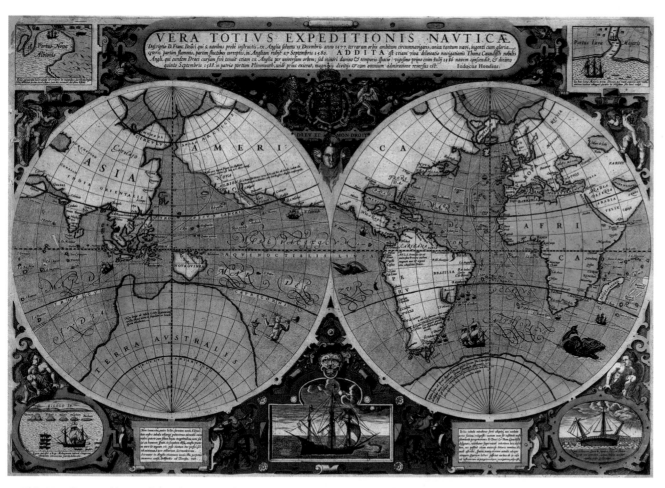

➤ This Hondius world map from about 1595 shows routes around the world of Sir Francis Drake between 1577 and 1580, and Sir Thomas Cavendish between 1586 and 1588.

THE NAMING OF AMERICA

Italian Amerigo Vespucci (1454–1512) made several voyages to the New World between 1497 and 1507, first for Spain and later for Portugal. His account of a first voyage in 1497 was probably untrue. It is believed his real first voyage, to what is now Brazil, took place in 1499. That was the first voyage to bring Europeans to continental South America.

Vespucci is the first person who used the term "New World" to refer to the land he had reached, unlike Columbus, who firmly believed he had reached Asia. For many years, people thought that Vespucci had named America after himself, but researchers later determined that it was not his idea. In a book called *Cosmographie Introductio* (*Elementary Geography*), published in 1507, German professor Martin Waldseemuller wrote:

> *But now these parts have been more extensively explored and another fourth part has been discovered by Americus Vespucci . . . wherefore I do not see what is rightly to hinder us from calling it Amerige, or America—i.e., the land of Americus, after its discoverer, Americus, a man of sagacious mind, since both Europe and Asia have got their names from women.*

In his map accompanying the book, Waldseemuller also used the term "America."

Though it was only a suggestion, by someone who did not even know Vespucci personally, the name caught on with geographers. By 1515, the name America appeared in a booklet that accompanied a globe made by Johann Schoner. In 1538, the names North America and South America appeared on Mercator's map of the world, the first time the two continents were identified separately. The name caught on, forever cementing Amerigo Vespucci's place in history.

➤ Nineteenth-century image of Amerigo Vespucci arriving on the continent that would become known as South America.

Rhode Island after himself) created a map that showed Manhattan Island for the first time; Father Marquette and Louis Joliet mapped the Mississippi River from 1672 to 1673; and Robert LaSalle explored the Mississippi River from 1679 to 1682.

The great explorers had a passion for discovery but also a desire to earn fame and fortune. Today, most of them are remembered not because of vast fortunes, but because they expanded the geographical knowledge of the New World.

➤ This early-18th-century map shows California as an island.

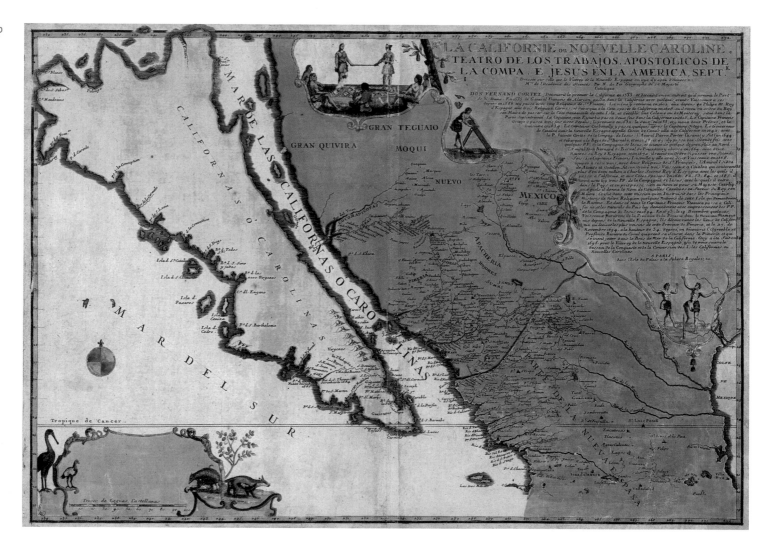

THE FOUR-COLOR CHALLENGE

A SOUTH African mathematician named Francis Guthrie was coloring a map of English counties in 1852 when he first came up with the Four-Color Theorem. This theorem said that you can take any blank map and, using only four different colors, shade in the countries so that no two adjacent countries are the same color. This theorem was too difficult to prove before computers but was finally proved in 1976.

You'll Need
➤ Photocopier
➤ Pencil
➤ Eraser
➤ 4 different colored pencils or crayons
➤ Blank white paper

This is both a mathematical and logical map challenge. Using only four colored pencils or crayons, color in each of the lower 48 states so that no two adjacent (bordering) states are the same color. When two states meet only at a point but do not share a border, such as Utah and New Mexico, they do not count as adjacent.

Make a photocopy of the US map on this page. First, use a pencil to mark what color you intend to use for each state—R (red), G (green), B (blue), and Y (yellow), for example. Start from Missouri and work in all directions from there. For a more challenging task, start from the West Coast and work your way east. If you make a mistake, erase the letter and try again. Once you are certain you have done a state correctly, you can color it in.

Next, you can put the Four-Color Theorem to another test. On a blank piece of white paper, draw imaginary countries of any size and shape. See if you can come up with an arrangement of imaginary countries that would disprove the Four-Color Theorem.

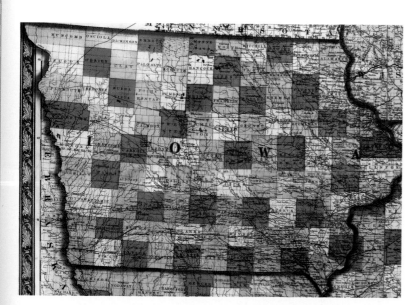

➤ This 19th-century map of Iowa's counties was tinted using only four colors.

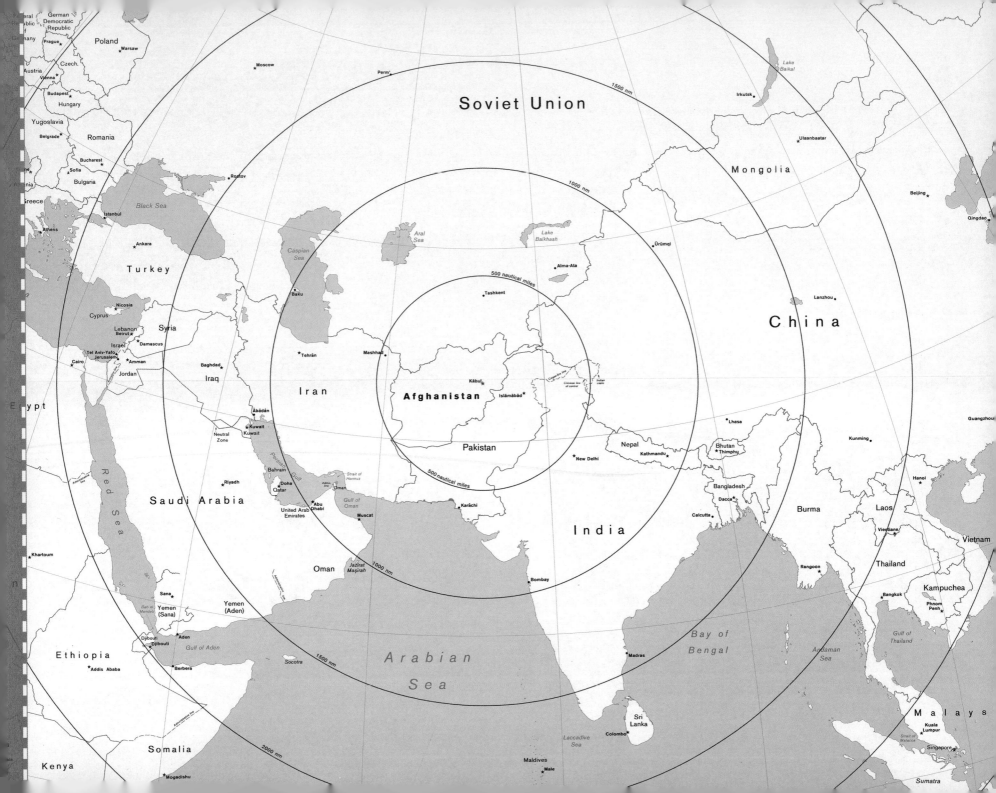

MAPS AND GLOBES:
Representing the Earth

2

IF A globe, round and three-dimensional, is a fairly accurate representation of the earth, then how can a map, something that is flat and two-dimensional, also be accurate? Take a piece of paper and try to fold it neatly into a ball. It can't be done, can it?

For centuries, mapmakers have faced a dilemma: how to accurately represent points on a ball onto a two-dimensional surface.

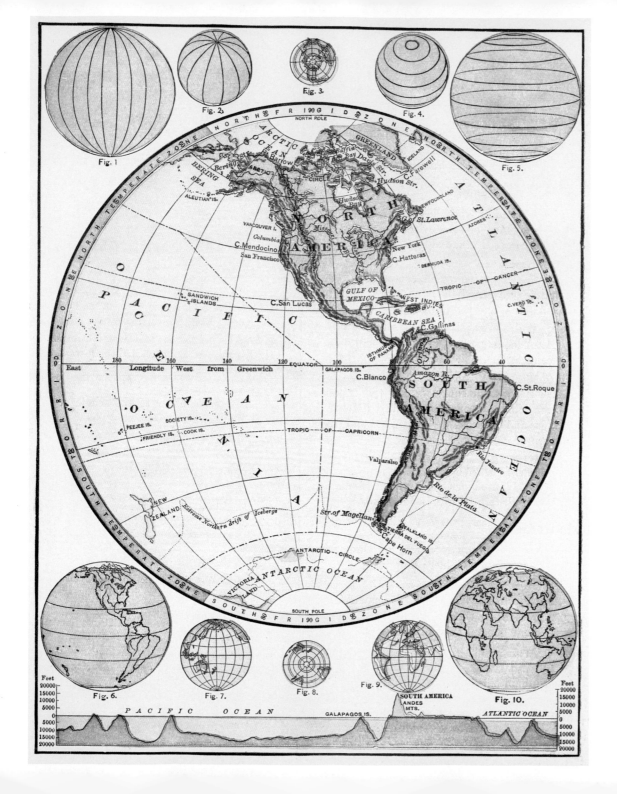

Poles and Parallels

IF THEY were to be completely true to physical reality, maps and globes would show only the size and shape of landmasses and water bodies of the earth. But that would not be very helpful. Readers need reference points to tell each other where a particular place is located on the earth's sphere.

The ancient Greeks believed the earth was a sphere and were the first to come up with a system of reference points for the sphere. Though the system has been refined over the years, we have held onto the essentials of the ancient Greek system.

The earth's *axis* is an imaginary line passing north/south through the center of the earth, around which our planet spins. The *poles* are the two extreme ends of the axis. The globe also has five important *parallels* around it (and perpendicular to the axis). One is the *equator*, the line that divides the earth into two halves, Northern Hemisphere and Southern Hemisphere. The *Tropic of Cancer* and the *Tropic of Capricorn* run parallel to the equator, each exactly 23½ degrees away from it. The polar circles (*Arctic* and *Antarctic*) also run parallel to the equator, at 66 degrees and 33 minutes. (Each degree can be further broken down into 60 smaller units called minutes, and each minute can be broken into 60 seconds.)

➤ Elements of the artificial sphere, 19th century.
Courtesy of NOAA

An invisible line called the *prime meridian* passes through the two poles and divides the earth into Eastern and Western Hemispheres. *Longitude* is the distance from the prime meridian, measured in degrees. *Latitude* is the distance from the equator to either of the poles.

Since ancient times, mariners set out in great sailing ships upon trade routes between Europe, Asia, and Africa. With limited navigational tools, they worried about getting lost and hugged the coastline to keep land in sight at all times. By the 15th century, great voyages of discovery were taking place across the Atlantic and Pacific Oceans. The best tools mariners had at that time were instruments to help determine latitude, or how far north or south a ship was on the imaginary grid of lines parallel to the equator. By measuring the angle of the sun and stars above the horizon, sailors could determine if they were heading toward Brazil or Iceland.

Unfortunately, there was still no way to determine longitude—how far east or west a ship was located. Knowing latitude alone did not tell a ship's captain how much longer the voyage might take. Poor winds and bad storms could set a ship back several days and there was no way to predict them. What if the crew was getting restless? Would the food supply last long enough? When would the ship hit land? Should the sailors give up, turn around, and head home? The vastness of the oceans made longitude crucial to navigators in search of new worlds and shorter trade routes.

➢ A map from 1600 shows a ship sailing off the coast of Cape Verde, Africa. In the days before longitude could be found at sea, ships hugged the coast as long as possible. Note the birdlike sea monster in this image.

Finding Longitude

SEVERAL EUROPEAN countries offered prizes to the first person who could discover a reliable method to determine longitude at sea. If there were a simple way to know the time on the ship versus the time at the home port, then it would be easy to determine longitude. But that meant having two clocks that would keep accurate time on board a pitching, water-drenched ship—one set upon leaving the home port, and one set at sea at noontime, when the sun reached its highest point in the sky. The bulky, inaccurate clocks of the day did not have the ability to keep correct time for weeks on end. A difference of several minutes could throw off the longitude calculation considerably, and that would be both useless and disastrous, stranding a ship in the middle of nowhere.

The Italian scientist Galileo had an idea in the early 17th century. Using his newly invented telescope, he discovered that the moons of Jupiter had eclipses. He realized that if he could make a chart of when the eclipses happened, a sailor could simply observe at what time the eclipse happened at sea, then refer the chart to see when it was supposed to happen back at the home port. By calculating the difference in times, the navigator could then figure out the ship's longitude. It seemed to be a perfect plan! But Galileo was never able to come up with a good way for the seamen to view the moons of Jupiter. An ordinary telescope would not be still enough at sea to focus on the tiny area of the sky where the moons could be found.

In 1675, King Charles II of England founded the Royal Observatory at Greenwich in an attempt to develop a system of longitude. In 1714, the Eng-

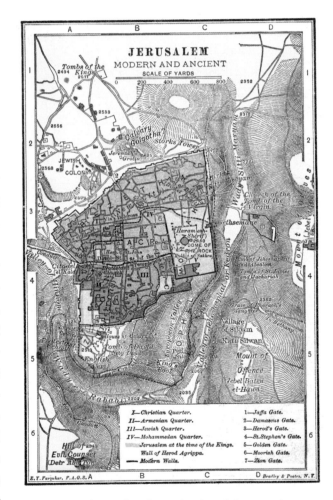

➤ This map of Jerusalem from 1896 has alphanumeric coordinates.

lish government offered a prize of 20,000 pounds (millions of dollars in today's currency) to anyone who could devise a method for tracking longitude. In the 1720s, a clockmaker named John Harrison finally solved the problem by developing a precise clock, or *marine chronometer*, that would keep perfect time at sea.

Then came the problem of determining where to locate the prime meridian. Since locating 0 degrees longitude was an arbitrary decision (unlike latitude, for which 0 was set at the equator), several different countries claimed the zero or prime meridian. In 1884, an International Meridian Conference was held, and 22 of the 25 nations attending (including the United States) agreed to use Greenwich, England, as the prime meridian of longitude (0 degrees).

While most large maps include latitude and longitude, some maps instead use a coordinate system for easy reference. This is especially true for maps of cities, where the differences in latitude and longitude are small. The 1896 map of Jerusalem on the previous page has an alphanumeric reference system, with numbers on the vertical axis and letters on the horizontal axis.

Which Way Is North?

THE EARTH sphere consists of both a northern and a southern hemisphere, but one possible reason we live in a north-oriented world is because the earliest geographers and mapmakers were from the Northern Hemisphere. As a result of this bias, our maps are oriented so that north is facing the top.

If you were to head north from wherever you currently are, you would eventually wind up at the North Pole. The North Pole is called *true north*. *Compass north*, which points to the magnetic north pole, is rarely the same as true north. This difference between true north and magnetic (compass) north is called *magnetic declination* or magnetic variation. This declination varies from year to year, and it also varies by your location, depending on shifts in the earth's magnetic fields. In 2010 in the United States, the magnetic declination varied from –19 degrees in Maine all the way to +18 degrees in Washington State, with a line of 0 degree declination running through several states near the Mississippi River.

Here's how magnetic declination works. A declination of –10 degrees means 10 degrees westerly, while a declination of +10 degrees is 10 degrees easterly. For example, if in your location the declination value is +15 degrees, and according to your compass you are heading on a bearing of 90 degrees, you are actually heading on a true course of 105 degrees. If your navigational directions refer to "true," that means you have to compensate for the declination when you navigate.

➤ A compass on a nautical chart from 1911 shows the declination for that year—in this case, 15 degrees.

Though we don't often use a compass to navigate around land, for hundreds of years, the compass has been the most reliable way to navigate a ship. A ship's captain can use a chart before sailing to figure out what heading or headings he or she needs to use during the journey. Modern compasses often include an adjustable base plate to allow for easy declination correction.

Political and Cultural Geography

THE TOPOGRAPHY of the earth and the pinpointed coordinates of different locations are not the only concerns of geographers. People and geography are closely linked, so social and political features and facts are also very important in the study of geography. Geographers are interested in where people settle, how they harness the resources of the planet for agriculture and industry, and what political boundaries they create.

Most maps have lines that show the political geography of the world, marking boundaries between continents, countries, provinces, states, counties, townships, villages, and congressional districts. Though these boundaries are artificial—you won't see them on the ground outside—we are so used to seeing them on maps that a map without political boundaries seems naked and shapeless to us.

Within a country, the inhabitants make geographical distinctions that outsiders may not make. These distinctions are based on many factors, including political boundaries and physical location as well as cultural and topographic similarities and differences. For example, look at the map of Nievre on page 28. Nievre is one of the 86 *départments* of France in 1851. This département is broken up into four *arrondissements*. The arrondissements are indicated by the green, yellow, and orange colored lines on the map. Each arrondissement is broken into *cantons*, a total of 25 for the département of Nievre. Distinctions such as these are mainly found on French maps, but not on maps of France drawn in other countries.

The distinctions we make within a country may be strictly political, or they may also be cultural. Geography affects culture because it affects how people live. People from the mountains live very differently than people from the desert, for example. The climate, resources, and natural surroundings of a place influence our behavior and customs.

We may consider anyone from Germany to be simply German, but within Germany, people from different regions of the country are seen as being unique. People in mountainous, forested Bavaria have a different cultural and regional identity from those who live in the flat, industrial areas along the Rhine River. Similarly, when we think of France, we typically don't think of geographical breakdowns, except perhaps the French Riviera. But the French make geographical distinctions between Brittany and Burgundy, and between Normandy and Nice, for example. The same is true for England, where someone from Yorkshire is seen as distinct from someone from Devonshire. The huge country of China is a good example of geographical variation. We have some hints of it from China's different regional cuisines such as Szechuan, Cantonese, or Hunan. But there are at least 12 different languages spoken in China, each one having several different regional dialects.

Within the United States, we recognize several distinctly different geographical regions, including the West or East, South or North. Sometimes we break it down further, into Northeast, Mid-Atlantic, Midwest, Southeast, Southwest, and Northwest. We make these distinctions based on a number of things, including the physical geography of the area and the dialect of the people. Even within each individual state, we sometimes make distinctions such as "upstate" and "downstate." Depending on the shape of the state, special geographic terms may be used. For example, in Florida, Texas, and Alaska, people refer to the "panhandle," a narrow strip of land. Californians refer to people from "the Valley."

COMPASS NAVIGATION GAME

WITH only a compass, navigation on land or at sea can be simplified. But the key is to know how to properly use a compass and how to follow directions.

YOU'LL NEED
➤ A friend
➤ 2 magnetic compasses

Take a friend to a park or a wide open space. Bring two compasses. To correctly use a compass, you need to hold it level, at about waist height. Try to keep the compass at least several inches away from anything metal.

To properly read the compass, first turn the dial until the degree bearing you wish to head in is aligned with the direction-of-travel arrow on the outer casing. Next, move your body until the red end (north) of the metal needle is aligned with the red orienting arrow on the inside of the dial. Then, walk in the direction of the bearing you have "dialed" (the direction-of-travel arrow), making sure to keep the red end of the needle steadily aligned with the orienting arrow.

Have your friend turn around while you go first, following the directions below. (Note: For the purposes of this game, you don't need to steer a "true" heading, just a compass heading.)

Mark your starting point by sticking a pencil into the ground. Set the compass to a heading of 60 degrees and take 10 steps in that direction. Next, change your heading to 150 degrees for 20 steps. Then go toward a heading of 320 degrees for 15 steps. Next change your heading to 20 degrees and go 5 steps. Finally, change to a bearing of 260 degrees for 25 steps. Secretly mark the spot where you wind up.

Next, have your friend follow the same directions, starting from the same point. How close did your friend get to your ending spot?

In many cities, residents make clear distinctions between neighborhoods, including "uptown" and "downtown," or "east side" and "west side." Each city has a geographical identity as a city, but within it, each neighborhood has its own identity in relation to the rest of the city. Though every town is laid out differently, the old saying "from the wrong side of the tracks" came from places where railroad tracks marked the end of a "good" neighborhood and the beginning of a "bad" one, away from the center of town and toward the more industrial or poor area.

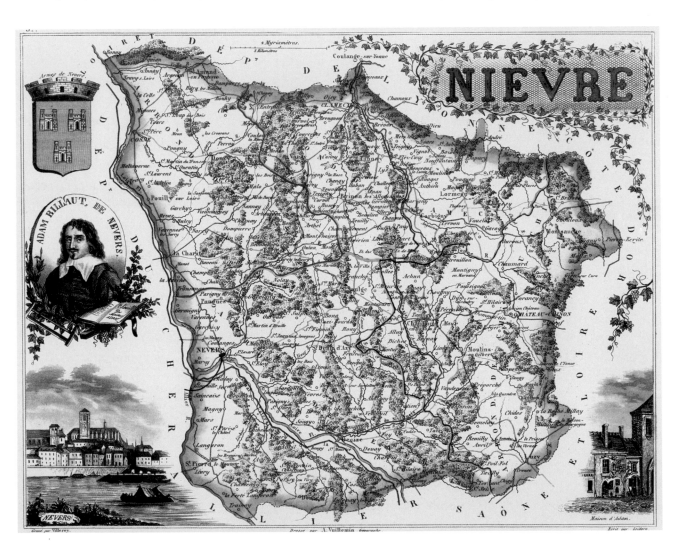

➤ An 1851 map of Nievre départment, France.

Mapping Human Geography

MAPS CAN be used to graphically show all kinds of information about people and geography. All you need is some information about different locations, and you can map the statistics to show the distribution of almost anything. Human geography includes the distribution of population, languages spoken, religions, disease and mortality, agriculture and livestock, industry and manufacturing, wealth, and more.

For example, if you have the data, you can plot on a map which states have the greatest percentages of senior citizens, brown cattle, two-story apartment buildings, silver mines, or jelly bean factories. The numbers alone aren't always useful, but when numbers are plotted onto a

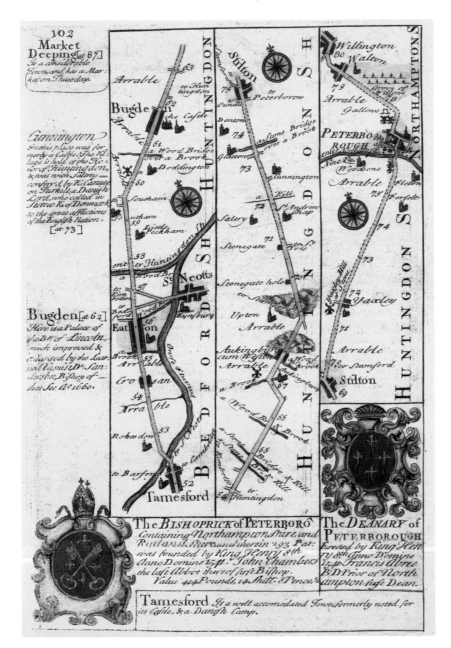

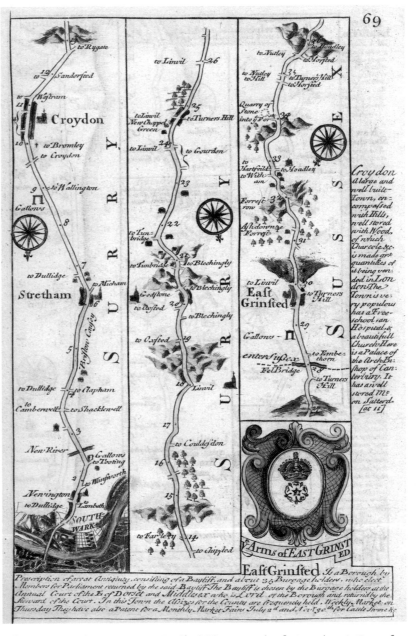

➤ These 1720 maps show roads in the area of Peterboro and Croydon, Surrey, England, and East Grinsted, West Sussex, England. The maps also feature descriptions of the areas' sights and landmarks. ("Bethlem Hospital was Originally a Mean House in ye Suburb of ye City for ye Maintenance and Cure of Lunaticks.")

READING MAPS

THERE is no such thing as a typical map. There are many different types of maps. The most common type (and one that you have probably used with your family) is the road map. It shows political borders of states and counties, roads and highways, and cities and towns, as well as a few other features. However, even road maps must be deciphered to be read correctly.

All maps use some form of key. For example, on a road map, lines of different thicknesses and colors may be used to show different sizes and types of roads such as interstate highways and state and county roads. Different sizes of lettering may be used to mark towns of different sizes. The mapmaker must decide how best to relay information so that the map's audience will be able to easily read it. A road map is no less complicated than a map showing rainfall totals over a 100-year period; it is only because we are used to reading road maps that they seem simpler. Just as auto-mobile drivers need to navigate using road maps, boat and ship captains need to read special depth charts to navigate coastal waters.

Though many maps show current data only (population, political party registration, etc.), sometimes data is accumulated over a wide range of years to show an average. In the first map below, mean (average) annual rainfall in New York State is shown over a 75-year period (1826–1900). The second map shows rainfall over a 30-year period (1961–90). Study the notes on each map and

➤ Maps of rainfall in New York State, 1826–1900 and 1961–90.

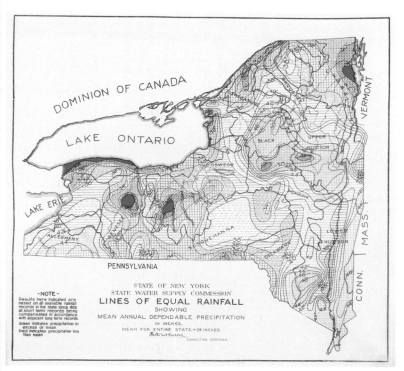

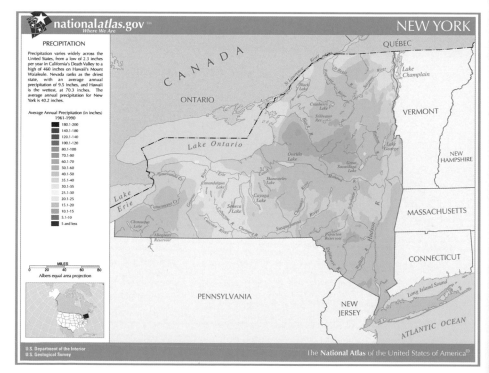

30

then try to answer the following questions:

1. What is the highest average rainfall in the state during each period?

2. What is the lowest average rainfall in the state during each period?

3. What are the main differences between the 19th-century rainfall totals and the 20th-century rainfall totals?

4. What differences between the graphic information on the two maps make it more difficult to compare them?

These maps provide only data, not the reasons why the patterns exist. To understand more about the differences in rainfall, you would need to cross-reference a topographic map and know basic facts about meteorology.

map, interesting patterns appear about where people or animals or industries are concentrated in a country. This information can be shown on a state level or broken down to county or other levels.

Maps showing the concentration of human population, natural resources, crops, or livestock, can become outdated quickly. The world is changing fast. Populations are increasing in some places and decreasing in others. Resources that were once plentiful have become depleted. The number and total acreage of farms around the United States continues to decrease.

➤ Map showing the population density of the United States in 1890. The purple areas were most densely populated. The uncolored areas had fewer than two people per square mile.

WET AND DRY MAP OF MICHIGAN, JANUARY 1, 1915.

➤ Wet and dry map of Michigan in 1915. Black denotes "wet" counties, where alcohol could be sold; white denotes "dry" counties, where alcohol could not be sold.

Because of this constant change, it is very useful to look at maps of the same thing over time, on a decade-by-decade basis. This is a good way to examine trends and try to predict the future. For example, in 1940 there were about 25 million milk cows in the United States. By 2000 the number had dwindled to about 9 million. Major agricultural changes have occurred in the last 20 years. In 1990 there were about 367 million bushels of oats grown in the country, and by 2005 this number had decreased to about 115 million bushels. On the other hand, in 1990 3.8 million bushels of flaxseed were grown, versus almost 20 million bushels of flaxseed in 2005.

Even those things you might think would remain stable, such as rainfall amounts and average temperatures, do not remain constant anywhere around the globe, as climatic trends change over the decades.

Customized maps can be created to show almost any type of information—for example, guinea pig owners by state, or political party registration for places with altitudes over 5,000 feet, or whatever may interest you.

Maps are also used to demonstrate a point. For example, the Anti-Saloon League, a group dedicated to making the sale of alcoholic beverages illegal, published a yearbook in 1915 showing the progress of its efforts around America. The book shows a map of each state, with the "wet" counties (where the sale of alcoholic beverages was allowed) colored black and the "dry" counties (where the sale of alcoholic beverages was prohibited) not colored.

The Geography of Health

MAPS ARE especially useful visual aids in helping scientists solve important problems. Scientists can use maps to analyze public health issues, from obesity to the incidence of heart disease. Studying the patterns revealed when health data is mapped can help epidemiologists, the scientists who study diseases and epidemics, figure out why certain deadly diseases are common in certain areas and how and why they spread. The map on the next page shows the frequency of deaths from typhoid fever according to the 1900 census. The data alone would reveal the number of deaths in different locations throughout the country, but only upon mapping can you really note and study the patterns that appear.

Sometimes maps can help reveal things that may not seem obvious. The typhoid map shows that in 1900 the rate of typhoid deaths in the Southeast was more than twice the rate in the Northeast. You might think typhoid would be more common in cities, where population density is high. But this map helps demonstrate the true difference between the occurrence of the disease in rural and urban areas in 1900. In states where the urban population was more than 60 percent of the total, the death rate per

100,000 was 25. Compare this to states in which the urban population was less than 10 percent of the population, where the death rate from typhoid fever was 67 out of 100,000. Though it is true that disease typically spreads faster in urban areas, typhoid fever is usually spread through dirty water supplies. The water in cities around the turn of the 20th century was typically safer to drink than that in rural areas. If the data on the map were broken down even further, it would reveal that typhoid fever is more abundant along rivers and streams, especially if they are used to supply drinking water to local populations.

The more precise the map data is, the more scientists can benefit from it. Public health officials are usually careful to gather as many details as possible for epidemics. For example, the maps on the next page show the location of typhoid cases in the city of Winnipeg, Manitoba, Canada. The first map shows occurrences of the disease during the outbreak of August and September 1904. The next map shows the location of typhoid cases during a second outbreak, in the months of October, November, and December.

Using this type of information, scientists can determine the possible reasons for an outbreak. In the case of Winnipeg, the first outbreak was in the poorer sections of the city. Scientists determined that these typhoid cases were largely the result of direct contact with infected people and infected flies. The second outbreak happened in a wealth-

ier area of the city and was the result of temporary pumping of water from the polluted Assiniboine River on October 10. This residential district happened to be near the location of the Assiniboine Pumping Station, which drew the water from the river.

An understanding of the disease and how it spreads has helped reduce typhoid deaths to nearly zero. Today, there are only about a few hundred cases of typhoid each year in North America, and the majority of those are people who acquired typhoid while traveling overseas. Sadly, more than

➤ Map showing typhoid fever deaths in the United States in 1900.

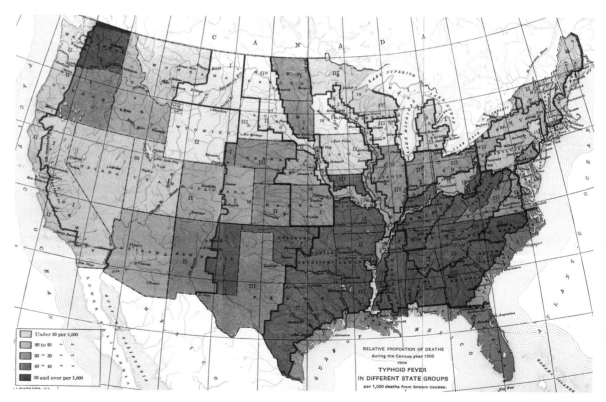

RELATIVE PROPORTION OF DEATHS
during the Census year 1900
FROM
TYPHOID FEVER
IN DIFFERENT STATE GROUPS
per 1,000 deaths from known causes.

Under 20 per 1,000
20 to 29 "
30 " 39 "
40 " 49 "
50 and over per 1,000

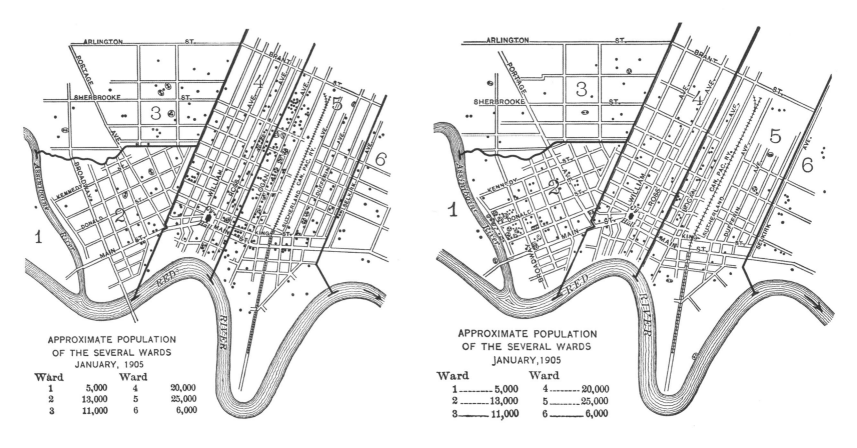

➤ Maps of Winnipeg, Manitoba, Canada, showing typhoid fever deaths during the August/September 1904 outbreak (LEFT) and during the the October/November/December 1904 outbreak (RIGHT).

21 million people elsewhere in the world suffer from typhoid every year.

Maps are currently being used to examine clusters of cancer cases around the country and determine the cause of these geographical cancer hot spots.

Map Projections

SINCE THE earth is a sphere, a globe is the only truly correct picture of the world's geography. But it would be inconvenient to rely only on a globe to learn about the geography of the world. To see each of the states in detail, for example, the globe would have to be large and heavy.

Flat maps are much more convenient because they are smaller, lighter, and cheaper. But these types of maps have to meet one important challenge—taking something that is located on the three-dimensional surface (the earth's sphere) and showing it on a two-dimensional (flat) surface, such as a piece of paper. To do this, the

POPULATION DENSITY MAP

POPULATION statistics, like many other statistics, are not very revealing until they are mapped. In this activity you'll map the population of Oregon's counties in the year 2000.

YOU'LL NEED
➤ Photocopier or scanner/printer
➤ Pencils, crayons, or markers in a variety of colors (see key)

➤ Physical map of Oregon or the West Coast of the United States

Make a photocopy of the Oregon map on this page, making it as large as you can. Using the population data from the 2000 US Census and the colors in the key, color the counties on the map according to their populations. The darker colors will represent the more highly populated counties.

Looking at this purely political map you've created, it is hard to tell why some counties are so populous while others are not. Now compare the county population map you've colored to a physical map of the state of Oregon. What are the elevations of the most populous counties compared to those in the more empty counties? In which counties are the biggest cities in Oregon located?

Key

0–5,000	= Yellow
5,001–10,000	= Orange
10,001–50,000	= Red
50,001–100,000	= Purple
100,001–500,000	= Brown
500,001 and up	= Black

➤ The counties of Oregon.
Courtesy of Cartographic Research Laboratory, University of Alabama

Population Data from the 2000 US Census

Baker 16,741; Benton 78,153; Clackamas 338,391; Clatsop 35,630; Columbia 43,560; Coos 62,779; Crook 19,182; Curry 21,137; Deschutes 115,367; Douglas 100,399; Gilliam 1,915; Grant 7,935; Harney 7,609; Hood River 20,411; Jackson 181,269; Jefferson 19,009; Josephine 75,726; Klamath 63,775; Lake 7,422; Lane 322,959; Lincoln 44,479; Linn 103,069; Malheur 31,615; Marion 284,834; Morrow 10,995; Multnomah 660,486; Polk 62,380; Sherman 1,934; Tillamook 24,262; Umatilla 70,548; Union 24,530; Wallowa 7,226; Wasco 23,791; Washington 445,342; Wheeler 1,547; Yamhill 84,992.

earth's curved surface has to be projected onto two dimensions. Places such as cities are small when compared to the entire earth, so earth's curved surface isn't a major issue when mapping them. For a map showing the world, a continent, or a country or large state, however, projecting the three-dimensional area onto a two-dimensional piece of paper is a challenge.

The oldest map projection, known as the *gnomonic projection*, is said to have been created by Thales, a sixth-century-B.C. Greek mathematician. Other ancient projections include the orthographic and the stereographic, both known over 2,000 years ago. These early projections more or less showed the earth as it would appear from space. In other words, you could create these types of projections by holding a globe at any angle and drawing exactly what you see on a piece of paper. These projections are therefore distorted by the mapmaker's perspective.

Whatever projection is used, however, it is useless unless the geography shown on the maps is also accurate. As map accuracy improved during the age of exploration, navigators and explorers needed a projection that would better help them in their travels.

Gerardus Mercator (1512–94), a pioneer in mapmaking and globe making, created just the thing for these for navigators. The *Mercator projection*, introduced in 1569, imagines that the earth sphere is placed into an upright cylinder, points on the sphere are projected onto the cylinder's wall, and the cylinder is then rolled out flat. The resulting world map is rectangular. The only place where a Mercator projection is not distorted is along the equator, where distances are true and correct. Minimal distortion occurs within 15 degrees north or south of the equator, but beyond that, the

➢ Gerardus Mercator in a 1595 engraving.

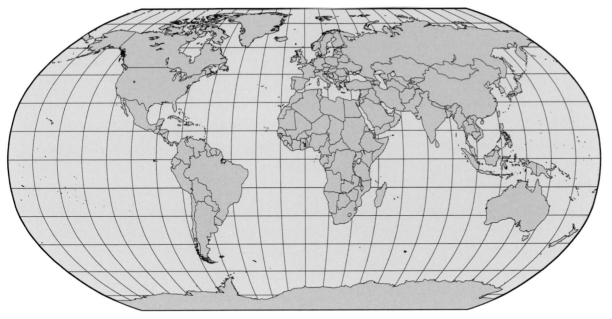

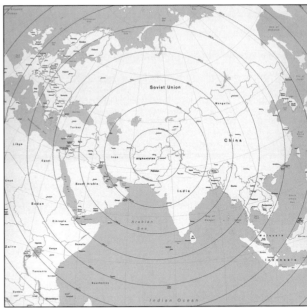

distortion is more pronounced the farther north or south you go.

The Mercator projection is most useful for sea navigation, because the directions are true even though the distance is distorted. If you are at a certain latitude on the coast of England and you want to sail to the Bahamas, you only have to set your compass to a heading according to the map and you will eventually reach the Bahamas.

Many new types of map projections have been created since the Mercator projection; the possibilities are nearly endless. One commonly used projection is the Robinson projection, introduced by Arthur Robinson in 1963. This projection pre-

sents the earth in more of a capsule shape, which gives more accurate sizes and shapes for places closer to the North and South Poles.

Another useful type is the conic projection, in which the earth sphere is projected onto a cone that is then rolled out flat. This projection is used in many atlases to depict the states of the Union, for example. The Azimuthal equidistant projection, which has its roots in the orthographic projections of ancient times, shows a view of the globe as seen when looking down (at a 90-degree angle) on a particular city or location; distances are accurate only from the centerpoint outward, not between two random points on the map.

➤ LEFT: Computer-generated Robinson projection of the earth. *Courtesy of Cartographic Research Laboratory, University of Alabama*

➤ RIGHT: Azimuthal equidistant projection centered on the city of Kabul, Afghanistan, created by the CIA in 1980.

MAP PROJECTION EXPERIMENT

ONE of the biggest challenges of mapmaking is to accurately project the spherical surface of the earth onto the flat surface of a map. In this activity, you will see for yourself some of the challenges of map projection.

YOU'LL NEED
- ➤ Black and blue permanent markers
- ➤ Inflated beach ball
- ➤ Globe
- ➤ Scissors
- ➤ Cone-shaped coffee filter
- ➤ Thumbtacks
- ➤ Foamcore board, about 12 inches square
- ➤ Drafting compass
- ➤ Pencil
- ➤ String
- ➤ Black felt-tip pen
- ➤ Ruler

With a permanent marker, draw an equator around the center of the beach ball. Mark the North and South Poles.

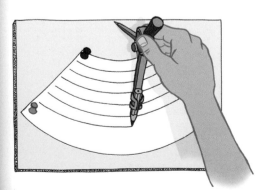

Using a globe as reference, draw approximate outlines of each of the continents on the beach ball. Mark them by name and do the same for the oceans.

Deflate the beach ball and use the scissors to cut it from pole to pole (longitudinally) through the Pacific Ocean. Try to spread out the flattened beach ball on the ground and see how difficult it is to accurately show the earth on a rectangular piece of paper.

If you'd like to experiment more with the concept of projecting a sphere onto a flat map, try this:

Cut a cone-shaped coffee filter at its seam. Tack it to a piece of Foamcore board. Use your drafting compass and pencil to draw several lines of latitude, each ¼ inch apart. Use string to measure the length of the top arc and then the bottom arc—lay the string along the arc, mark the end point with the felt-tip pen, and then measure the distance. Divide both measurements by 20. Using the pen, mark the distance of each of the 20 segments on both pieces of string. Lay the string against the length of each arc and transfer the points to the coffee filter. Next, use a ruler to connect your lines of longitude. You now have a rough idea of the principle behind the conic projection.

Map Scale

IF YOU'VE ever owned a little toy car or built a model of a car from a kit, chances are you have an understanding of *scale*. For these toy cars to look like the real thing, their designers had to create them to scale—each part of the car (the door, the headlights, the wheels, and the exhaust pipe, for example) is made in a correct size relative to the others. If the parts were not to scale, the toy car would look quite odd and not like a miniature version of the real thing.

Most maps also have a scale, a set ratio of map distance to actual distance. Scale can be expressed in three different ways. Some maps feature only one, and others show the scale in all three ways.

The first method of explaining scale is the representative fraction. A representative fraction scale of 1:50,000 means that one map unit equals 50,000 actual units. So one inch on the map would equal 50,000 inches (or 4,166.7 feet, about three-quarters of a mile). Similarly, one foot on a map of that scale would equal 50,000 feet (about 9.5 miles). A map at this scale would be a very close-up map, perhaps showing a particular city or county. On the other hand, a map with a scale of 1:2,000,000 would mean one inch equals about 31.6 miles. This scale might be useful in a road atlas of a large state such as Montana. A map showing the continental United States on a 17-inch-wide piece of paper would require a

> Bar scale.

scale of 1:12,000,000 (roughly one inch to 190 miles). A map of the entire world drawn on a sheet of paper 17 inches wide would require a scale of 1:100,000,000, where every inch is equal to 1,600 miles. Imagine how difficult it would be to draw a scale map of the solar system. The distance between the sun and the inner planets is tiny compared to the vast distance between the sun and the outer planets.

The second method of expressing scale is the written method, where the map would actually say "One inch equals 1,600 miles."

The third and most common scale is a bar scale showing inches and miles on a bar, one above the other. This allows the user to easily calculate real distance.

It is easy when using a map to rely strictly on measured distances to figure out how far apart two places are—say Denver, Colorado, and Reno, Nevada. If you look at a map and measure the distance, it is 790 miles. However, map distances can be deceiving. If you got in a car and drove from Denver to Reno the most direct way possible, it would be a 993-mile trip, a difference of more than

ATLAS AND THE ATLAS

Atlas was a Greek mythological figure whose Titans were at war against Zeus's Olympians. After the Titans lost, Zeus condemned Atlas to holding up the sky—the celestial sphere—for eternity.

In the 16th century, Gerardus Mercator was the first one to use Atlas's name in conjunction with a book of maps, and it stuck. For hundreds of years, maps were primarily found in books, not as single, stand-alone pages. These hardcover atlases were often quite large, twice or three times the length and width of this book, for example. The pages, or plates, of the best quality atlases were made of thick paper and contained a map on only one side. Atlases were also very expensive; only the wealthiest people could afford them.

> A 45-foot-high statue of Atlas stands at Rockefeller Center in New York City.

Many of the earliest atlases wound up in the collections of major university libraries around the world, where many remain today. As the decades and then centuries passed, the old atlases that were still in circulation became rare, and the maps they contained grew quite valuable. Antique dealers soon realized they could make more money by cutting the atlases apart and selling the maps separately. In other cases, parts of an old atlas might have been damaged by water or mold, so some of the remaining maps were saved and removed. In any case, it is rare to find an intact atlas from the 18th century or earlier.

200 miles. It is uncommon to be able to get from one place to another along a straight line. And, due to geography, traveling the same distance in different places is not equally simple. Traveling 100 miles through winding mountain roads is more difficult and takes longer than 100 miles on a flat, straight highway—though it might not take as long as 100 miles through a busy, traffic-congested city.

Finally, if you come across a map that says "Not drawn to scale," what does that mean? It means that the relative distances shown on the map are not accurate representations of real distances. Suppose you read a map (that says "Not drawn to scale") showing a hotel on Second Street one inch away from Main Street, which is in turn an inch away from Highway 44. In reality, the hotel and Main Street might be 500 feet away, while Main Street and Highway 44 might be a mile apart. These kinds of maps are intended to give only an idea of a place's location—to get to the hotel, you have to leave the highway at Exit 30, get to Main Street, and then turn onto Second Street. When using a map like this, you will have to watch carefully to make sure that you don't miss any turns.

Mapmaking Methods

THE FIRST maps were one-of-a-kind pieces produced on stone, clay, metal, or papyrus. Until the invention of the printing press in 1454, copies of a map had to be made by hand.

One of the early methods of mass mapmaking was through the use of inked woodcuts. Woodcut maps were

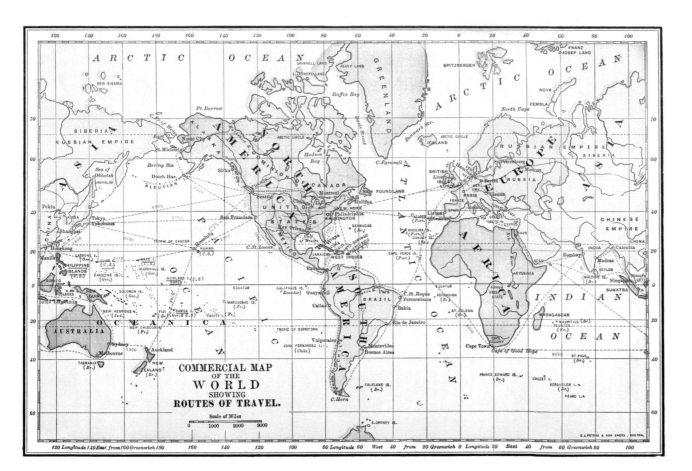

➤ This world map, from about 1900, uses a Mercator projection, with a scale of one inch equaling about 3,500 miles.

DRAW A MAP TO SCALE

A MAP is meant to be a miniature representation of how a place actually looks in full size. The scale of a map depends on the area of the place being depicted. A map of your local neighborhood, for example, might require a scale of 1:1,000 (one map inch = one thousand real inches); whereas a map of the United States might have a scale of 1:7,500,000 (one map inch = 7.5 million real inches). This activity, from an old schoolbook, is one that kids used to study scale at the turn of the 20th century.

YOU'LL NEED

➤ Yardstick or tape measure

➤ Graph paper (8½ by 11 inches)

➤ Pencil

➤ Magnetic compass

➤ Calculator

Measure the length and width of your desk or table, then the length and width of your graph paper. How can you represent the desk on this size of paper? You must draw it smaller, to scale,

keeping the exact proportions. See if three inches representing one foot works. If so, draw it to scale. Then, using the magnetic compass, place points of direction on the drawing, showing which way is north.

Next, measure the full length and breadth of your classroom (or bedroom, or living room). Choose a scale and transfer these measurements to a new sheet of paper. Measure the distance from each wall to the nearest corner desk in a straight line. Place the four points. Measure the length and width of floor space occupied by pupils' desks. Place points and sketch in light lines. Divide this space to represent aisles and desks. Measure the distance between desks. Find the number of aisles, the number of rows of desks, and the number of desks in each row. Locate the teacher's desk, the door(s), and the windows. Use the compass to place points of direction; also place a star to indicate your own desk.

IS THE MAP TO SCALE?

MOST maps will say whether they are to scale or not. In this activity, you'll have a chance to figure out whether a particular map was drawn to scale.

YOU'LL NEED
➤ Ruler
➤ Calculator
➤ Notepad and pen
➤ Piece of thin string, about 15 inches long
➤ Scissors

The map on the right shows the Roosevelt Raceway and surrounding area as set up for the Vanderbilt Cup Race of 1960. No scale is given. To determine whether the map is drawn to scale, you'll have only a few clues with which to work.

Clue 1: A lap is 1.5 miles (7,920 feet).

Clue 2: The longest straight section of track is 2,350 feet.

Clue 3: The actual distance from the intersection of the Meadowbrook Parkway and Old Country Road to the

intersection of Merrick Avenue and Old Country Road is about 6,750 feet.

The first step is to determine if the track itself is drawn to scale. Use the ruler to measure the longest straight stretch of track. Divide 2,350 by your measurement. The result will be the number of feet per inch. Write the result on your notepad.

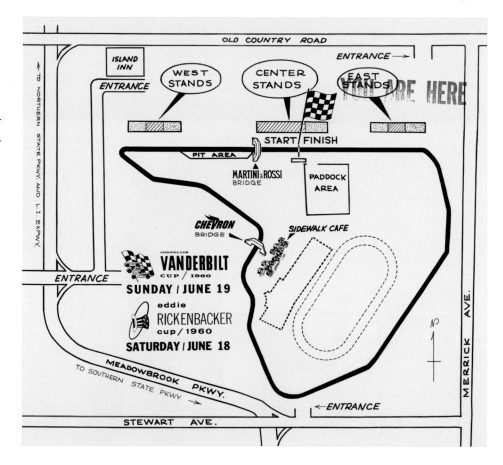

Now lay the string as closely as possible along the outline of the entire track. Cut the extra string so you have a piece of string that is exactly as long as the track. Now use the ruler to measure the string. Divide 7,920 by your measurement. Write the result on your notepad. If the track is drawn to scale, the result should match the scale you got earlier (give or take a slight error depending on how accurately you have used the string).

Now that you know whether the track itself is drawn to scale, the next step is to figure out if the track is to scale with the roads surrounding it. Use the ruler to measure the distance from the intersection of the Meadowbrook Parkway and Old Country Road and the intersection of Merrick Avenue and Old Country Road. Divide that number into 6,750. Is this result anywhere near the number(s) you got when you measured the track? Is this map to scale?

➤ Vanderbilt Cup racetrack, Long Island, New York, 1960.

42

cut in reverse, or mirror image, to make a correct print. They were also cut "in relief" so that the parts not to receive ink were cut away, leaving only the lines and various elements to be shown raised (and capable of receiving ink). Modifications to a woodcut map were tricky.

The 16th and 17th centuries were golden years for mapmaking. Several of the finest cartographers worked during that time. Besides Mercator, there was Sebastian Munster (1488–1552), a German cartographer who updated the maps of Ptolemy in 1540. In 1544, Munster published the first edition of his *Cosmographia*, an enhanced woodcut geography of the world with images of historic events, scientific information, city views from around Europe, as well as the customs and legends of different peoples. This popular work was reprinted in many later editions and was translated into several languages. Munster had devised a new method for adding place names—towns, mountains, rivers, and so on—to woodcut maps. While the features themselves were still carved into the wood, instead of carving out the names, which would be very difficult to change, a blank space was chiseled onto the woodcut, and metal type spelling out the name of each place was inserted in the empty space. In this way, the map could easily be reused, even if the place names changed later.

Other prominent mapmakers were the Dutch cartographers and publishers Jodocus Hondius (1563–1612) and Jan Janssonnius (1588–1664). In the early years of the 17th century, Hondius bought the plates to Mercator's *Atlas* and updated them, publishing a new version. Janssonnius, who was married to Hondius's daughter and is better known as Jansson, carried on the Mercator/Hondius tradition, publishing even newer versions of the atlas.

Woodcut maps began to fall out of favor later in the 16th century with the growing popularity of a new method for making maps: using engraved copper plates instead of wood. Lines on woodcut

➢ Hand-colored Munster woodcut plan of Basel, Switzerland, from his book *Cosmographia*, 1550 edition.

MAKE A CONTOUR MAP COME TO LIFE

TOPOGRAPHIC *maps* show the physical features of the earth. They show elevation through a series of lines called *contour lines*. First used on maps in the 18th century, contour lines are useful because they show how steep a slope is and give us an idea of what terrain is like. If you were to go on a hike, you'd want to have a contour map with you to see how difficult the trails are. All points along a contour line are the same eleva-tion above or below sea level. In low-lying areas, the contour lines may represent increases of only 20 feet. In more hilly or mountainous zones, they might represent 100 feet or more. Contour maps also show the elevation at certain benchmarks, or key spots, such as hill or mountain peaks.

ADULT SUPERVISION REQUIRED

YOU'LL NEED
➤ Pencil
➤ At least 25 sheets of tracing paper
➤ Scissors
➤ 2 sheets of 20-by-30-inch Foamcore board
➤ Hobby knife
➤ Glue
➤ Modeling clay (optional)

The contour map on the right shows an imaginary island. Use a pencil to trace the 20-foot contour line on this map onto a piece of tracing paper. Do the same for each of the other contour lines, using a new spot on the tracing paper for each. (Use a new sheet of paper when necessary.) Use scissors to cut out each of the contours. Place them atop the Foamcore board and draw the outline of each one with your pencil.

Have an adult use a hobby knife to cut out the shapes of each of the contours. Assemble the contours according to the original map, using glue to set each layer atop the one beneath. When you are done, you'll have a physical representation of the island shown in the contour map.

To get an even better idea of the true shape of the land, you can apply modeling clay to the contours, making sure the clay follows the Foamcore board outline as closely as possible.

➤ Topographic map of the Boston, Massachusetts, area, 1900.

maps tended to be thick because there was a limit to how finely one could carve out details in relief. The process for copper plates was the reverse of that used for woodcuts; copper plates were engraved so that the incised lines would hold ink. This meant that very fine lines could be reproduced.

Copper was the metal of choice because it was soft, which made engraving easy. (Gold and silver are also soft, but too expensive.) A mapmaker would start with a smooth and bright sheet of copper a little larger than the size of the finished map. Lines would be engraved with a wooden-handled, fine-pointed steel tool called a burin. The deeper the engraved line, the more ink it would hold, and the bolder the line on the finished map. Different people might be hired to do the line work, lettering, and shading. The entire plate was covered in black (or other color) ink and then wiped off with a rag. The flat surface would come clean, but the grooves would hold the ink since the rag could not penetrate them. The plate would then be applied to a sheet of paper with great pressure, causing the ink in the grooves to be transferred to the paper, creating the map. The mapmaker would have to be careful, because any accidental scratches on the copper plate would hold ink and make black marks on the printed map. A 19th-century copper plate press could be used to create between 500 and 700 impressions (probably of various maps) per day; some mapmaking businesses had several of these machines.

Once the map was printed, the various countries or areas on the map were hand-colored with watercolors, so the lettering and lines of the map could still be seen underneath. Women were often hired to do the coloring, and they would use camel hair brushes to apply colors as directed. Some maps required only "lining," or faintly coloring the borders of states or countries, while others required "washing," or painting entire areas uniformly with a particular color. The women who colored the maps needed much practice to become experts. In 1830s

➤ This is a 1635 copper-engraved, hand-colored map of Germany designed by Jansson. For centuries, any color on maps had to be added by hand, as the printing process could not easily handle more than one color.

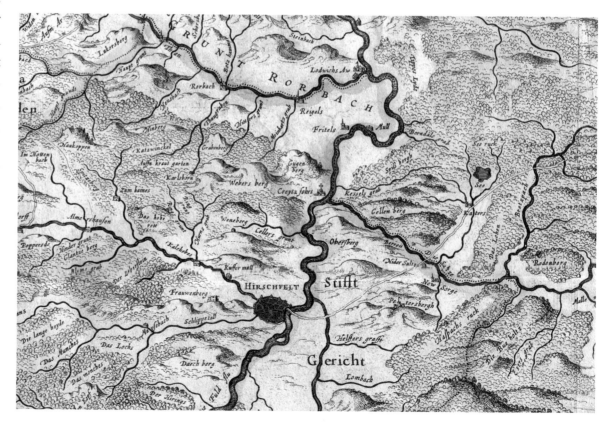

ENGRAVE A MAP

MAP engravers using wood or copper plates had the difficult task of engraving everything as a mirror image (backward), so the resulting impression on paper would be a correct image. In this activity, you'll try engraving a map in reverse.

YOU'LL NEED
➤ Sheet of aluminum foil, 12 by 12 inches
➤ Piece of cardboard, 8½ by 11 inches
➤ Tabletop (standing) mirror
➤ Dull pencil

Place the sheet of foil over the piece of cardboard and wrap the edges around so that the cardboard is completely covered.

Select a map in this book. Set a standing mirror on a table and hold the map to the mirror. Using a pencil, engrave the map as it appears in the mirror. Draw as many of the map's details as possible, including borders, rivers, and cities.

When you are done, engrave the map's name (for example, Map of Massachusetts) and your name backward under your drawing.

To see how your map turned out, unwrap the foil from the cardboard and turn it over.

➤ A man engraves a copper plate for a topographic map, 1937.

America, a young woman could earn between three and five dollars a week as a map colorist.

Map printers would often reuse older engraved copper plates when they published new maps. Plates could be altered to change place names, country borders, or geographical details, and it was cheaper and easier than engraving an entirely new map. Even 100-year-old plates were reused with only minor changes. If an entire section of a map became outdated, that part of the plate could be beaten from the back and repolished on the front so that it could be reengraved, while still leaving the rest of the plate's details untouched. Also, after a few hundred prints, the lines of an original plate might become worn, making recutting (reengraving the original lines) necessary.

The quality of a map consists of two different parts: the accuracy of the geographical information and the quality of the printing. The quality of maps from this period—the fineness of the lines and the map's overall appearance—was due largely to the skill of their engravers.

In the early 19th century, steel plates were introduced and soon became the favored medium for creating maps. Steel is harder than copper, so finer lines can be incised. The steel plates themselves also last a lot longer than the copper ones, without losing detail.

Another new method introduced in the 19th century would become the most popular one for printing maps. Called *lithography*, this method involves drawing map details in reverse on a stone (or on a piece of paper that would then be transferred to a stone).

Lithography is a chemical process, unlike the mechanical processes of using woodcuts or copper or steel plates. The lines and points of the map are drawn on a special two-inch-thick polished lithography stone (a kind of slate). A special chemical ink is used to draw the map. There are many variations of this ink, but they all contain beeswax, soap, and lampblack or a colored ink. Other ingredients include turpentine, shellac, and tallow. This greasy ink is applied with a steel pen and seeps into the stone. Besides being applied in liquid form, the ink can be made into a kind of chalk with a pointed tip, so fine lines can be drawn.

After the drawing is completed, the stone is treated with an acidic solution. As long as the stone is still damp, the chemical reaction of the acid with the stone causes the ink to be repelled. Next, the greasy ink is removed with a form of turpentine, leaving behind marks where the lines were drawn. These greased areas continue to absorb or attract ink. The prepared stone is then rolled with lithography ink, and paper is inserted. When prints are made from the inked lithography stone, only the areas with the greased lines (to which printing ink sticks) will print, while the rest of the stone will repel the ink.

In 1905, a mapmaking innovation called photolithography was introduced. It used lithographic stones containing photo impressions, and many multicolored impressions could be made from one inking.

Modern-day mapmaking is a precise science. A cartographer may be given a distinct set of rules to follow depending on the type of map being drawn. For example, in the early 20th century, the US Forest Service issued detailed instructions for making its maps, noting the correct tints of each color used in the maps. For example, to make the proper map color for areas with a density of 25,000 to 50,000 board feet of lumber per acre, you would have needed to mix four parts Higgins brown ink, two parts Sanfords green ink, one part Pomeroys yellow ink, and seven parts water.

➤ Color separation freehand scribing is done by a US Geological Survey cartographic specialist in California, 1957. Once the work was done, the map could be photographed to create a negative for reproduction.

GEOGRAPHY AND THE NEW WORLD

3

DURING THE 17th century, as the waves of explorers who visited the New World sent favorable reports back to Europe, a steady stream of settlers from Europe began to enter the Americas. The European population of the American colonies rose from about 350 in 1610 to 50,000 in 1650. By 1700, there were 250,000 settlers in the English colonies of North America, and many thousands more lived in New France and New Spain.

The Settling of North America

THE EARLIEST arrivals to North America were the Spaniards who founded missions in California and Florida, followed by English who settled at Jamestown, Virginia, beginning in 1607, and Plymouth, Massachusetts, in 1620. Other Europeans came to North America during the early 17th century, including French, Swedish, and Dutch settlers. Europeans arriving on the East Coast found land with geographical features and climate similar to where they had lived before. There was fertile farmland, forests, hills and modest mountains, rivers and streams. Much of what is now known as New England looked to these settlers very much like old England.

During the 17th century, European settlement remained for the most part east of the Allegheny Mountains, but during the 18th century, brave souls began to venture west. They discovered there were a few passes cut by rivers through the mountains, including the Delaware River at the Delaware Water Gap between Pennsylvania and New Jersey; the Potomac River at Harpers Ferry, West Virginia; and the James River in Virginia, as just three examples.

As more and more settlers journeyed westward through these and other passes, territories became populated enough to earn statehood. The Northwest Ordinance of 1787 said that a territory must have a population of at least 60,000 to be considered for statehood. Kentucky joined the Union in 1792, Tennessee in 1796, and Ohio in 1803.

➤ The southeastern part of North America, 1657. Spanish and French possessions are shown. What modern-day states would fall on the area shown in this map?

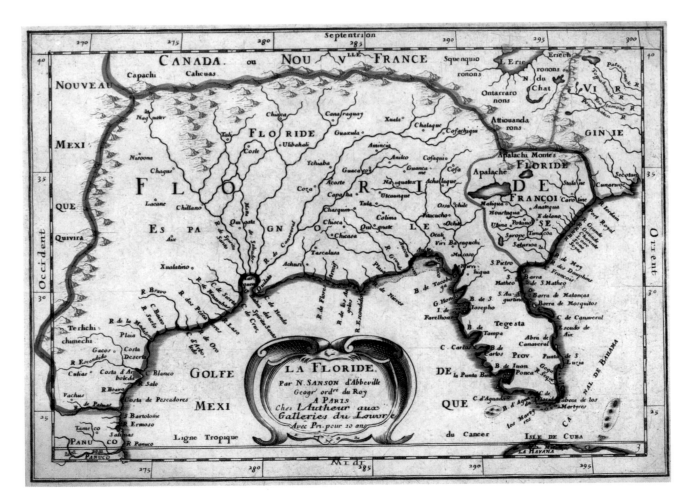

The biggest geographical development in the history of the young country was the 1803 purchase of 925,000 square miles of land west of the Mississippi River. The vast territory in the middle of North America was bought from France for 15 million dollars, partly because the French ruler Napoleon was looking for money to fund his army.

Some were critical of the deal at the time, but after Lewis and Clark's expedition west (1804–06), the fertile Louisiana Purchase land was settled rapidly. Louisiana became a state in 1812, Indiana in 1816, Mississippi in 1817, and Illinois in 1818. Another major American land purchase came in 1819, when the United States made a deal with Spain to buy Florida for five million dollars.

Geography played a big role in the 1844 presidential campaign. The vast Oregon Territory, extending from 42 degrees latitude to 54 degrees 40 minutes latitude, had been jointly administered by the United States and Great Britain since 1818. Eventually, both parties wanted to settle on a final boundary between US and British territory. US Democratic presidential candidate James Polk took a hard-line approach: he wanted the entire Oregon Territory for the United States. He even adopted a campaign slogan of "54-40 or Fight!"— a reference to the latitude of the northern border of the territory. Polk beat challenger Henry Clay in the election, but negotiations with Britain pro-duced an agreement in 1846 in which the United States settled for the 49th parallel of latitude as the border with Canada.

➤ A map of the Oregon Territory in 1841, with the original border and the final boundary highlighted.

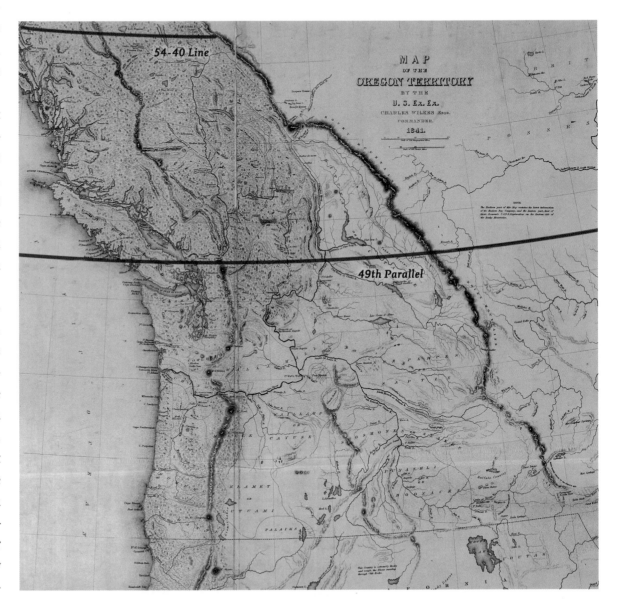

CREATE A GEOGRAPHICAL PROFILE

MAPS are excellent tools because they contain so much information about a place that you can easily compare it to other places. Though the greatest variation can be seen between locations that are hundreds or thousands of miles apart, there is often microvariation between very close places. For example, an area near the ocean may be an average of 10 or 15 degrees cooler in the summer than one only a couple of miles away from the water.

In this activity, you will collect your own rainfall, snowfall, and temperature data where you live, and compare to data from friends and family members who live between 1 to 100 miles away.

You'll Need
➤ 5 friends
➤ Outdoor thermometer
➤ Pail or bucket
➤ Journal or notebook and pencil
➤ 12-inch plastic ruler
➤ Map of the area

Select five or more classmates, friends, or family members who live within 100 miles of your home. Mark their locations on your map. Each person will need the other materials listed here and will perform each step of the activity. First, place the outdoor thermometer in a shady location. Place the bucket in an open spot that has no trees or other obstructions above it.

Each participant should agree to take temperature readings at least two or three times a day (at the same times each day) for at least two weeks and record them in a notebook. The date and amount of precipitation from each rainfall or snowfall event also should be noted in the journal. Use the ruler to measure the precipitation in the bucket, and then empty the bucket so it is ready for the next rainfall or snowfall.

After the observation period is over, gather the readings from the different locations into a table.

The Geography of Slavery

As the United States added territories, it created political complications. As early as the beginning of the 19th century, slavery was shaping up to be a major issue nationwide. Most of the Northern states had abolished slavery by that time, but most of the Southern states still allowed it. With the United States continually growing in size, the question of whether slavery would be allowed in new territories was a thorny one.

The addition of new land caused serious concern among members of Congress. Those representing the Southern states did not want restrictions placed on slavery in territories that were rapidly earning statehood. The Missouri Compromise of 1820 allowed Missouri to enter the Union with no restrictions on slavery, while Maine was to be admitted as a free state, without slavery. In addition, slavery would be prohibited in future states that lay north of 36 degrees 30 minutes in latitude.

The issue was not closed, though. As the United States continued to expand, slavery continued to be a sticking point. California was the next big challenge. By the late 1840s, the discovery of gold in the California Territory saw thousands of fortune seekers flood the area. Before long, California was eligible for statehood. With an equal number of free and slavery states in the Union at the time, California's antislavery constitution was seen as a possible roadblock to statehood. A compromise was reached in Congress where California would be admitted as a free state, but Utah and New Mexico could enter the Union however they pleased, as either free or slave states.

In 1854, the Kansas-Nebraska Act passed, allowing settlers in those territories to decide for themselves whether to allow slavery (contradicting the Missouri Compromise of 1820). Kansas was admitted as a free state in 1861.

Ultimately, the battle over slavery was one of the primary causes of the Civil War, which began just three months after Kansas became a state. The differences between "North" and "South" were based on geography as much as anything else.

Though there was already a very real sense of north and south in the country before the Civil War, this distinction was stressed even more during and after the war. The states that were part of the Confederacy are still thought of today as the South (Virginia, North Carolina, South Carolina, Georgia, Florida, Alabama, Mississippi, Louisiana, Texas, Arkansas, and Tennessee). Though Maryland and Delaware were slave states, they did not secede during the war, and today they are not considered as being in the South.

Among the last major changes to the nation's map was the absorption of the Indian Territory into Okahoma upon its statehood in 1907, and the addition of New Mexico, Arizona, Alaska, and Hawaii, the last states to join the union.

➤ This map shows Oklahoma Territory, around 1900. At the time, the eastern half was Indian Territory. Once Oklahoma became a state in 1907, the Indian Territory was negated.

Surveying and Land Boundaries in America

THE EARLIEST maps were only as accurate as the measurement tools used by their makers. The very first maps were drawn by eye, without the aid of any tools. But over time, better equipment was invented to help create more accurate maps.

Surveyors are the people who perform the precise measurement of land's natural features and

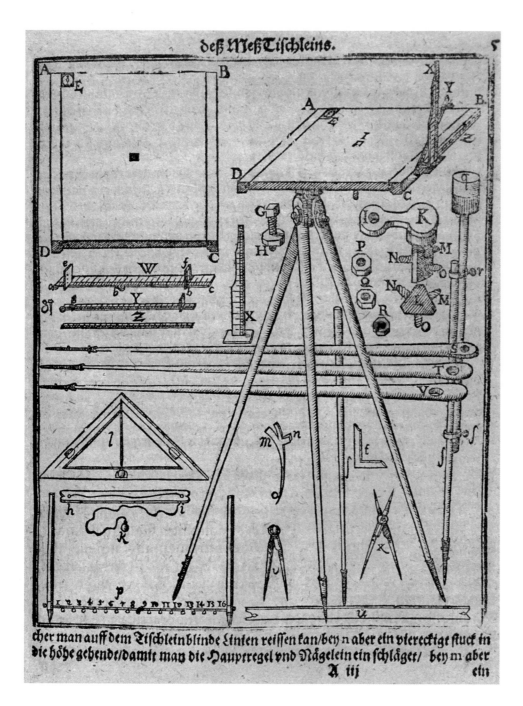

cher man auff dem Tischlein blinde Linien reissen kan/bey n aber ein vierecktge stuck in
die höhe gehende/damit man die Hauptregel vnd Nägelein ein schläget/ bey m aber
ein

A iij

man-made boundaries. When you buy a piece of property, a survey of the plot of land is required. This survey shows the exact coordinates of the land you are purchasing, and maps out the land in relation to neighboring land, including any landmarks such as walls, fences, buildings, or perhaps trees. It provides dimensions of the plot as well. The survey helps create an officially documented picture of the piece of land in case any disputes arise in the future. As years pass and changes are made to property—for example, if a new building is built or an old one gets an addition—then a new survey is required to show the changed conditions.

As American settlers moved west in the 18th century, the need for surveyors increased. The great numbers of settlers staking their land claims, exploring the country's natural resources, and building roads, canals, and railroads meant that better maps were needed.

Because the country was still very young, there were many questions and disputes over land. As people explored and settled in the westernmost states and territories, there were conflicts over who was entitled to the land and which land deed was the correct one. Another big reason for land disputes was the metes and bounds system of surveying that was used to mark property.

The *metes and bounds system* of surveying dates back to the early colonial days, and it is still used in

> Surveying equipment, 1630s. *Courtesy of NOAA*

the original 13 colonies and those states that were born from those colonies, including Maine, Kentucky, and Tennessee. It describes pieces of land using natural landmarks such as trees, rocks, rivers, and buildings as base points, using a "pole" (16 and a half feet) as a unit of measurement. Land disputes were common in the early days of the country, and the validity of surveys was sometimes questioned.

Some metes and bounds land dispute cases made it all the way to the US Supreme Court. In Kentucky in 1783, Henry Crutcher and John Tibbs registered ten thousand acres of land

> *beginning at a large black ash and small buckeye [tree] marked thus (I.T.) on the side of a buffalo-road leading from the lower blue licks [a naturally occurring salt deposit] a north-east course, and about seven miles north-east by east from the said blue licks, a corner of an entry of twenty thousand acres made in the name of John Tibbs et al ... running thence with the said Tibbs & Co.'s line due east sixteen hundred poles, thence south one thousand poles, thence west sixteen hundred poles, thence north one thousand poles to the beginning for quantity.*

Can you see where there might be problems? For example, what if two neighbors cannot agree on which "large black ash" is mentioned in the deed? A small black ash tree will become a large

one in 50 years, and then there might be two trees nearby. In fact, the defendant in this 1809 Supreme Court case argued that since the original survey of 1780, "there were many cabins, marked trees ... of which there remain now no traces, and which are now wholly incapable of proof as to what was their exact position ... a great change has taken place in the appearance of the country generally round ... great changes have taken place in the names of streams, roads and other objects."

Though some states still use the metes and bounds system, most of the United States uses the Public Land Survey System (PLSS), which dates back to the Land Ordinance of 1785 and the Northwest Ordinance of 1787. Each public domain state was laid out into a series of six-by-six-mile townships. Each township was then divided into 36 sections of 640 acres (one square mile) each. More divisions were made if necessary. A person could own an entire section, a half-section, or an eighth-section.

Boundary disputes are rare in these states because of the precision of the geometric system. The PLSS also made record-keeping easier, allowing detailed "plat" maps of land ownership for each section to be drawn. Most of the PLSS surveys were drawn based on an initial point. There are 37 different north-south reference lines called *meridians*, each one intersected by an east-west line called a base line. Therefore, when you describe the location of a section of land under the

BECOME A SURVEYOR

SURVEYS are necessary to mark property boundaries, whether personal (the line between your neighbor's yard and your own yard) or political (the border between two countries). Modern-day surveyors have sophisticated instruments that help them create highly accurate surveys, but the basic principles of surveying can be demonstrated using a few simple materials.

YOU'LL NEED
➤ Open space, such as a backyard, schoolyard, or park
➤ Hammer
➤ 4 dowels
➤ 2 magnetic compasses
➤ Heavy-duty tape measure
➤ 2 friends
➤ String, colored twine, or yarn (at least 200 feet)
➤ 45/45/90 drafting triangle (or a square piece of cardboard)
➤ Graph paper
➤ Pen or pencil

Find an open space at least 50 feet by 50 feet, where you can perform your survey. Pick a starting point (near the center of your space, if it is a small area), and hammer a dowel a few inches into the ground so it stands on its own. While standing next to the dowel you hammered into the ground,

take out one compass. Making sure the compass's red arrow stays pointing north, turn your body so that you are facing due west.

Hold the tape measure at the top of the dowel and have a friend pull the tape out for exactly 25 feet to the west. Have your friend hammer a dowel into the ground at that spot. Tie string from your dowel to your friend's dowel.

Place the compass on top of your friend's dowel. From that dowel, the compass should show that the string to the first dowel is due east. Next, from the second dowel, measure 25 feet due north, following the same process as before. Tie a string from the second dowel to the third dowel, at the same height as your first string. Double-check the direction by going to the third dowel

and sighting the compass along the string. It should be pointing due south.

Another way to check the accuracy of your dowels is to place a drafting triangle (or cardboard) at the intersection of the two strings and make sure they are at a perfect right angle. Continue the process until you have surveyed a perfect square.

Now, accurately record the square on graph paper and add other elements to the plot—sidewalk, trees, and so on—that might fall within, or just outside of, the square.

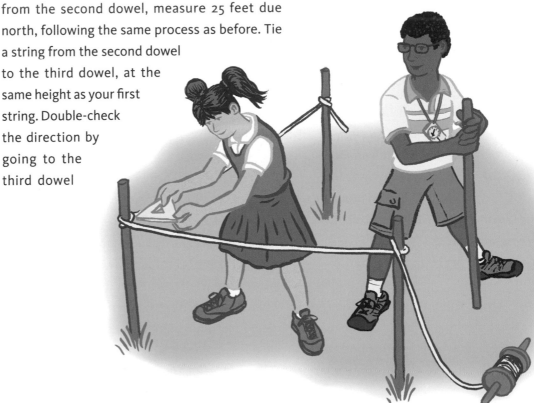

PLSS, you have to note whether it is east or west of the meridian and north or south of the base line. A PLSS description of a piece of land always starts with the state and name of the meridian and then gets more specific. An example of a typical description is: Montana, Principal Meridian, Township 24 North, Range 2 East, Section 2.

The Mason-Dixon Line

ONE OF the most famous surveys ever conducted was that of the Mason-Dixon Line, the border between Pennsylvania and Maryland. Though many people think of the Civil War and North versus South when they hear the words "Mason-Dixon," the line was part of a land dispute that started more than 150 years before the Civil War.

In the 1680s there were some issues with the original land grants made by the King of England to William Penn, the owner of Pennsylvania, and Lord Baltimore, the owner of Maryland colony. There was confusion about the real location of the border between the two pieces of land, because the grant said the border was at the 40th parallel (40 degrees latitude). This would place the boundary north of Philadelphia, which was part of Penn's colony.

There was also a dispute as to the ownership of the Delaware peninsula. A proclamation by governor of Maryland in 1722 split the land east-west.

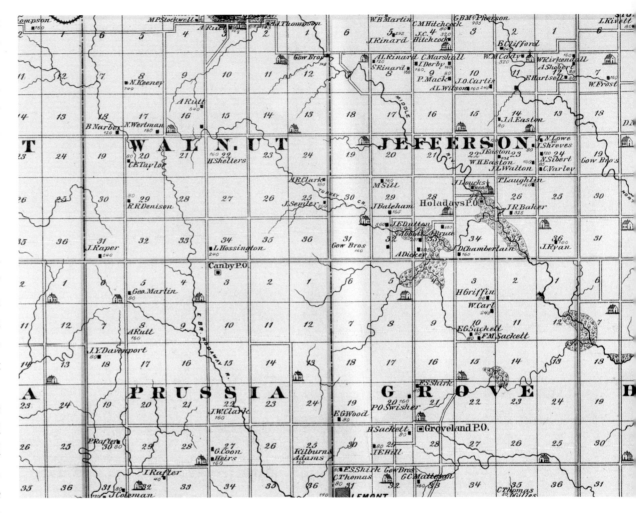

➣ Detail from a plat map of Adair County, Iowa, 1875.

Lord Baltimore did not agree with that, and lawsuits followed. In 1760, four surveyors (and many assistants) were appointed to resolve the issue. They spent three years before it was decided they lacked the skills to do the job correctly. The problem remained unresolved until expert surveyors were brought in from England. Charles Mason

> ABOVE: Mason-Dixon border map, published in 1768 in Philadelphia.

> LEFT: Mason-Dixon Line Marker in Adams County, Pennsylvania, photographed in 1950.

(1733–79) and Jeremiah Dixon (1728–86) arrived in Philadelphia in November 1763 and quickly had a small observatory built so they could determine the exact latitude of Philadelphia. Once they did this, they could proceed with their survey.

Mason and Dixon first surveyed the border with Delaware and then began marking the boundary between Pennsylvania and Maryland. They had stones, marked with a P on one side and an M on the other, placed every mile. Every fifth mile, a larger stone had Baltimore's coat of arms on one side and Penn's on the other.

In 1766, upon reaching the top of the Little Allegheny Mountain, the survey team met some resistance from the local Native Americans, who were skeptical of the strange scientific instruments the team carried. A treaty was negotiated and Mason and Dixon were allowed to continue their work, even bringing some natives with them as guides. By now the team had 30 surveyors, 15 axmen to chop trees, and 15 Native Americans (including chieftains).

A few months later, when they reached a place called Dunkard Creek at the bottom of a valley, they encountered a Native American warpath. At this point their escorts insisted that this was as far as they were allowed to proceed. Fear rippled through the survey team, and 26 of the surveyors abandoned the mission. Mason and Dixon also decided they could not continue without risking injury, so they finished their work at a point 36 miles from the western edge of the state. The rest of the line was surveyed by others from 1782 to 1784.

Place Names in North America

WHEN THE first colonists arrived in North America, they learned the names that Native Americans had given to places and geographic features. The natives were pushed away from areas where the Europeans settled, and often out of existence, so their place names were sometimes the only remaining trace of the original culture.

Though in some places colonists kept Native American names, in others they named their settlements after the places from which they had come. Many areas along the East Coast were named in honor of existing places: the states of New Jersey, New York, and New Hampshire, and the cities of New Britain and New London, Connecticut. Place names honored not only Great Britain but also locations throughout Europe: Athens, Georgia (Greece); Paris, Illinois (France); Vienna, Virginia (Austria). In fact, many locations adopted the same names. Besides Rome, Georgia, there are also Romes in Illinois, Indiana, Iowa, Kansas, Kentucky, Mississippi, Missouri, New York, Ohio, Oregon, Pennsylvania, South Carolina, Tennessee, West Virginia, and Wisconsin. In the state of Ohio alone, you can visit London, Manchester, and Oxford (England); Paris, Versailles, and Marseilles (France); Athens and Sparta (Greece); Rome and Venice (Italy); Moscow (Russia); and Warsaw (Poland).

Some towns on the border of two states have names that combine parts of each state's name. Examples include Calzona, California (California/Arizona); Calexico, California (on the Mexican border); Kanorado, Kansas (Kansas/Colorado); and Texarkana, Arkansas (Texas/Arkansas). There is also the curious case of Kenova, West Virginia, which straddles, Kentucky, Ohio, and West Virginia.

Still other places were named in honor of famous people. For example, the city of Charleston, South Carolina, was named after King Charles (as was the state; Carolus is the Latin name for Charles) and Madison, Wisconsin, after President James Madison. There are also Lincoln, Nebraska (Abraham Lincoln); Jackson, Mississippi (Andrew Jackson); and of course, Washington, D.C. (George Washington). Maryland was named after Henrietta Maria, the wife of King Charles; Georgia was named after King George II; and Williamsburg, Virginia, was named after King William III. Virginia itself was named after

Queen Elizabeth I; Albany, New York, was named after the Duke of Albany, who later became King James II; and Pennsylvania was named after its founder, William Penn.

All across the country, the mixed heritage of the settlers shows clearly through the names of its towns and cities. This mixture is often very diverse, even within a single state. In many parts of New York, you can find Dutch names mingling with English names and Native American names. In Wisconsin, you'll find German names such as Kronenwetter, Berlin, Rhinelander, and Germania; French names such as Fond-du-lac, Little Eau Claire, and Portage; and Native American names such as Pensaukee, Manitowoc, and Sheboygan mixed in among British names such as Medford, Dorchester, and Abbotsford.

Twenty-six state names are derived from Native American words or tribe names, and seven state names come from Spanish words or names.

In the West, towns popped up rapidly as railroad lines were constructed. Important settlers were likely to have a town named after them. In New Mexico, for example, towns were named after judges, clergy, senators, congressmen, army officers, railroad officials, pioneering settlers, railroad engineers, ranchers, merchants, and even a railroad mechanic.

American place names can be fun and even silly. There is a Santa Claus, Indiana, so named on Christmas Eve 1852 when, after months of discussion and debate, a child's cry of "Santa Claus!" inspired the town to pick that name. In 1950, Ralph Edwards, the host of a popular nationally broad-

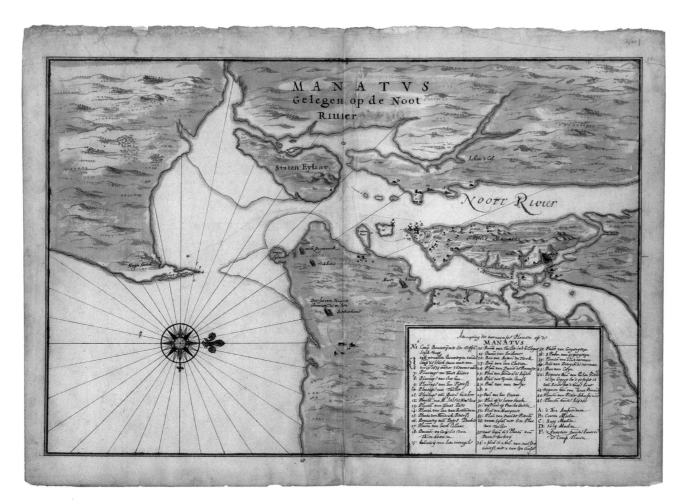

➤ This 1659 map of what is now New York City and its environs shows the Dutch and Native American origins of some of the names still in use today: Staten Eylandt (Staten Island), Conyi Eylandt (Coney Island), Helle Gadt (Hell's Gate), and Manatus (Manhattan). Note that north is not "up" on this map.

cast radio show called *Truth or Consequences*, asked if there was any town in America that was willing to change its name to honor the show. Officials in Hot Springs, New Mexico, were interested and put the matter up to a vote. It was approved 1,294 to 295, and the town officially changed its name to Truth or Consequences, New Mexico. Among many other silly place names are Fifty-Six, Arkansas; Bumblebee, California; Parachute, Colorado; Beer Bottle Crossing, Idaho; Oven Fork, Kentucky; Slapneck, Michigan; Alligator, Mississippi; Peculiar, Missouri; and Sandwich Landing, Nevada.

Settlement Patterns and Altering the Environment

THROUGHOUT HISTORY, people have looked for the best locations in which to settle. The best places were those located within easy reach of food (or where food could be easily grown), shelter, and a source of water. This is why many towns and cities were founded in coastal areas, or along rivers and lakes.

But even the best locations were not perfect. Land near rivers and along the coast is more likely to have natural marshes, swamps, and wetlands. Stagnant water can be a problem. Besides being breeding grounds for disease-carrying mosquitoes, these marshy areas are useless for building because the soft ground causes foundations to

PLACE NAME ORIGINS

THOUSANDS of American place names are based on European locations, because immigrants who founded towns often named them after the places where they originally lived. Because of the wide range of ethnic groups that settled the country, there is a great variety in US place names in.

In this activity, you will study place-name origins in states in different parts of the country.

YOU'LL NEED
➤ Road atlas or other detailed map of the United States
➤ Lined 4-by-6-inch index cards
➤ Pen/pencil
➤ French, German, Spanish, and Dutch dictionaries (optional) or Internet access
➤ Graph paper

Pick any state that you wish to study. Turn to the back of the atlas, where there should be an index of towns and villages shown on the map. List each of the categories given below on a separate index card. You may add any other categories you think are needed, such as "Miscellaneous" or "Unknown."

Now go through the list of your selected state's towns. Using dictionaries or researching on the Internet, try to fit each town into one of the categories on your index cards. (Hint: You can try to type the town name—both town and state—into a search engine. Sometimes, towns will have their own web page that gives information as to how the town got its name.) When you've completed your state, make a bar or pie chart on graph paper showing your results, and compare them with your friends' results for other states. Examples:

People's Names
Douglas, Clifton, Logan, Shirley, Madison, Crawfordville

Native American Names
Cohasset, Manchaug, Lenawee, Ronkonkoma, Manitowoc

Names from Other Countries
Dorchester, Paris, Albany, Rome

Spanish Language Names
San Jose, San Francisco

French Language Names
Coeur d'Alene, Des Moines

Descriptive Names
Crestview Hills, Morning Sun, Fountain City, Summit Lake, West Bend, Seaside

How Did It Get Its Name?

The town of Drumheller in Alberta, Canada, is known as the Dinosaur Capital of the World due to the rich fossil beds in the area. But how did it get its name? The story starts in the town of Mechterstadt, in the province of Thuringia, Germany, in the mid-17th century. A man named Hans Trumpfheller, born there in 1627, migrated several hundred miles west to the province of Hesse, Germany, and started a family. The Trumpfhellers lived happily in Hesse for about 100 years, before several members of the family decided to leave Europe and make a new start in America.

During the mid-18th century, several Trumpfhellers arrived in Pennsylvania and changed their name to Drumheller. Over the years, branches of the original Pennsylvania farming families spread out to different parts of the colonies. One branch of the Drumhellers moved to western Virginia and lived within sight of Thomas Jefferson's home, Monticello.

In the early 19th century, the family moved to Gallatin, Tennessee, which was still considered the frontier at that time. Soon after, in the early 1840s, the family moved to the Ozark Mountains near Springfield in southwestern Missouri. Following the California gold strike of 1848, three young Drumheller brothers decided to move west to find fortune. First went Jesse in 1852, then Tom, and finally Daniel Drumheller in 1854. The journey was long and perilous, but all three made it. The Drumhellers settled in California, Oregon, and Washington. They dabbled in ranching, prospecting, real estate, and local politics.

Early in the 20th century, Samuel Drumheller (son of Jesse) and his cousin Jerome (son of Daniel) were hiking in the Badlands of Alberta, 90 miles northeast of Calgary, Canada, when they came across coal in the cabin of one Mr. Greentree. They realized the potential of the land in the area and bought mineral rights. Samuel opened a mine. Legend has it that the name of the town was decided based on the flip of a coin—Greentree versus Drumheller.

It is amazing to think that most towns and cities in the United States have complex stories behind their founding.

➤ Drumheller, Alberta, Canada, in a 1930s postcard.

sink. Through the 19th and 20th centuries, countless acres of swamps in the United States were filled to make the land habitable.

Geographical problems don't stop people from settling. For example, low-lying parts of northern New Jersey are prone to flooding, yet thousands still live there. A lack of water sources did not stop people from settling in the desert, and a major earthquake fault line does not stop people from living in parts of California.

For thousands of years, people have been changing geography to suit their needs. In New York City, for example, settlement began at the southern tip of Manhattan Island in the 1620s and expanded farther and farther north as the city's population grew. But as the settlement moved north, the wilderness had to be tamed. Hills were leveled, swamps and ponds filled, and rock outcrops blasted away.

One obstacle to expansion was a large boggy area known as Lispenard Meadows. It was typically flooded by river water at high tides and was difficult to pass through due to the spongy nature of the soil. As settlement reached the area during the early 19th century, a huge amount of landfill (dirt and garbage brought in from elsewhere) was placed into the Meadows to level the land and make it habitable. The Collect Pond, on which local farmers used to skate in wintertime, was also filled in. In addition, landfill was dumped into both the East and Hudson Rivers to expand the width of

the island and even out the rugged shoreline. In the process residents created several extra blocks of land. Besides the dirt excavated from flattened hills, everything possible was used for fill: broken bricks, china, and even pieces of old ships. More than 25 percent of present-day lower Manhattan is actually built on landfill.

In 1811, a plan that mapped the rest of the island was approved. This plan was a simple grid of streets that did not allow for preserving any of Manhattan's natural features. It spelled the end for the rest of the hills, valley, marshes, and streams, with the exception of parts of Central Park, a large area that was preserved in the 1850s.

➤ Lispenard Meadows in Manhattan (New York City), seen here as it appeared in 1785, was a naturally low-lying geographical feature that was frequently flooded. It was eventually filled in so it could be occupied, and it is now a busy part of the city called Tribeca.

Historic maps of New York and other major cities around the United States show the changes to their topography over time. For example, before the nation's capital was relocated to Washington, D.C., the land there was nothing more than swamps and marshes.

There are hundreds of port cities around the country, located along bodies of water with an outlet to the ocean. Each one has seen many improvements over the years, mostly to accommodate and protect bigger ships and more marine traffic. Both dredging (digging out sediment from the bottom of a water body) and filling (dumping soil and garbage into the water to create land) have been used to change natural ports. Many ports have an "outer harbor" with deep waters and open access to the ocean, and an "inner harbor," a more protected area with shallower water. Sometimes the inner harbor is artificially created or enhanced by building jetties or other barriers to protect the ports from severe weather.

Throughout history, people have built canals to cut easier paths for transportation of people and goods. The Erie Canal in New York State, completed in 1825, connects the Great Lakes to the Atlantic Ocean, making it much easier to ship goods to the middle sections of the United States. Perhaps the most important change to world geography was the construction of the Panama Canal in Central America between 1904 and 1914. This canal allows ships to travel between the Atlantic and Pacific Oceans, a huge savings in time compared to when ships had to round the tip of South America.

Humans have also built dams to supply water and harness its power. In early-20th-century Massachusetts, planners decided that the Quabbin

➤ Atlantic entrance to the Panama Canal, 1914.

Valley in western Massachusetts, about 75 miles from Boston, was the ideal place for a reservoir to supply water to the big city. Unfortunately, there were four towns located in the valley that would be flooded. The towns' residents filed a lawsuit, took their case to the Massachusetts Supreme Court, but lost.

A total of 7,500 remains were moved from 34 local cemeteries and reburied elsewhere. Over 600 homes were moved, but many more were simply demolished. More than 35 miles of railroad were abandoned. As news of the coming flooding of the valley began to circulate in the 1920s, the

➤ RIGHT: The Quabbin Reservoir, seen here in a 1990s photograph, was created when the Quabbin Valley was flooded in the 1930s. Four towns had to be evacuated and destroyed to create this source of fresh water in western Massachusetts.

ALTERING OUR ENVIRONMENT

OR as long as people have been building cities, they have been changing the environment.

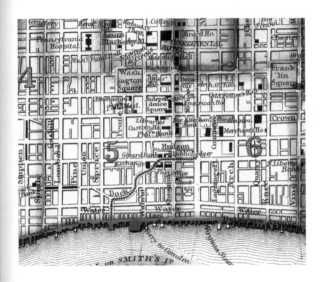

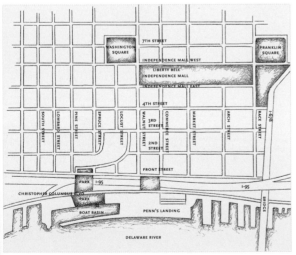

➤ Philadelphia in 1862 and now.

Look at the 1862 map of Philadelphia and then compare it to the present-day map of the city. Find the Independence Mall, where Independence Hall and the Liberty Bell are located, on today's map. Now try to find it on the 1862 map. If you have trouble, use other landmarks common to both maps to help you. It did not exist in 1862, did it?

Now find Delaware Avenue, along the Delaware River, on the old map. Can you find it on the new map? What has happened to the waterfront in the years since 1862?

What would you be able to say about an archaeological site found on Penn's Landing? Would it be from before or after 1862?

towns suffered. People and businesses wanted no part of a place without a future. Between 1920 and 1930, the population of the four towns decreased from 2,024 to 1,378, a 32 percent decrease. By 1935 the population had decreased to 1,119 as residents continued to find other places to live.

The towns were officially disincorporated on April 28, 1938, and a farewell party was held. Two dams were built. The flooding of the valley began in August 1939 and was finished seven years later, eliminating any traces of the towns of Dana, Greenwich, Enfield, and Prescott from the map. Unflooded land around these flooded towns was given to other nearby communities. Today, the Quabbin Reservoir holds 25,000 acres of water (415 billion gallons). It is a popular place for fishing and recreation, and home to a wide variety of animals.

The Quabbin project pales in comparison with one of the nation's most dramatic wonders: the Hoover Dam. The 6,600,000-ton dam at the border of Arizona and Nevada took five years to build. A total of 21,000 men worked on the dam between 1931 and 1936, using 5 million barrels of cement and 183 million pounds of steel to create the structure. Lake Mead, the reservoir created by the damming of the Colorado River, is 157,900 acres (or 247 square miles), making it the largest reservoir in the country.

Unlike the case of the Quabbin Reservoir, large numbers of people didn't have to move due to the flooding of the area to build the Hoover Dam. Few people lived there because the land was too dry. The dam solved that problem by using an existing river to create a source of drinking water.

Recently, people have begun to realize that while projects such as these are often necessary, too much change to the natural landscape is not good for the planet. Changing the ecosystem too much can hurt many plants and animals and upset the natural balance. These days, when construction projects are proposed near wetlands, builders often have to ensure the government that the wetlands will not be harmed. And if a project is to be built upon a wetland, the builder must "create" replacement wetlands nearby to make up for those that are destroyed or harmed.

Learning Geography

GEOGRAPHY AND maps change over time because country borders and place names change. Geographically, the land that made up the New World of colonial days is very different today. During the 17th and 18th centuries, and part of the 19th century, several countries had colonies in North America. The Dutch, English, French, Spanish, and Swedish all had settlements in parts of the continent.

Geography books usually are written from the perspective of the country that publishes them.

CREATE A ZONING MAP

As towns and cities grew during the 19th century, elected officials realized that people should not be allowed to just build anywhere as they had been doing. There had to be some rules about where different types of buildings—single-family residential, multiple-family residential, commercial, industrial, and institutional—could be located within a community. These rules are known as zoning laws, and they create zones for different types of buildings.

Is your neighborhood zoned? In this activity, you'll map out the uses of buildings in your neighborhood and see if there is a pattern.

YOU'LL NEED
- ➤ Graph paper
- ➤ Black pencil
- ➤ Colored pencils or markers (red, blue, orange, yellow, green, etc.)

With the help of an adult, walk or drive 10 square blocks in your neighborhood. Make a map of the neighborhood on graph paper, drawing each building as a square on the map. Assign each color to a type of building:

Red = school, library, hospital, museum, courthouse, town hall (institutional)
Blue = store or restaurant (retail)
Black = industrial (factory)
Orange = private home (house)
Yellow = apartment building or condominium
Green = park, playground

Color in a square for each building on your map. Can you see a pattern of colors? Are factories next to homes? Are stores close together? Are schools next to apartment buildings?

Take a trip to your town hall's buildings department or local library and find your town's zoning map. Does the map you drew match the zoning map you found?

Should a town be allowed to make zoning laws as it pleases? Why do you think your town is zoned the way it is? What changes would you make to your town's zoning laws to make it a better place?

Thus, geography students around the world tend to learn more about their own country and its possessions or colonies than they do about other countries. A French geography book from 1756 describes North America by talking first about New France (Canada and Louisiana), then about English possessions (New Scotland, New England, New York, New Jersey, Pennsylvania, Maryland, Virginia, and Carolina), and lastly Florida, New Spain (Mexico), and California. The book devotes 93 lines of text to describing the French colony of Louisiana but much less space to the English colonies—only 15 lines to New England, 14 lines to New York, 8 lines to New Jersey, and 5 lines to Maryland.

Though plenty of geography books were published during the 18th century, they were for older students. It was not until the 19th century that school-age children in the United States had to go to school. Once most children were attending schools, the number of textbooks increased dramatically. Geography was one of the main subjects 19th-century children studied.

Unlike kids of today, who are likely to have visited several states (and maybe several other countries), schoolchildren of the 19th century were unlikely to have traveled outside their town or community, much less their own state. Most 19th-century families did not take vacations, so there was no real reason for children to travel, unless their families migrated to a different part of the country.

Schoolchildren of this time learned about the geography of their country mostly through maps and schoolbooks rather than through firsthand experience. Among other things, 19th- and early-20th-century American geography textbooks focused on the crops and industries popular in the different regions of the United States. Because farming was so common in those times, children learned details of where and how various crops were grown, and where different types of livestock were raised.

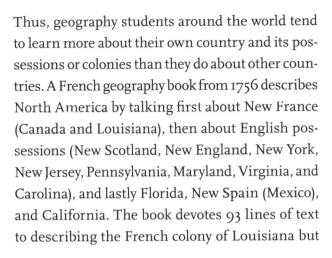

➤ Schoolchildren study a brook bed during an early-20th-century field trip.

In 1900, a child might have learned the details of where and how wheat, flax, and sugar beets were grown, and how maple syrup was made. One 1900 textbook told about making turpentine and gave details on how to grow sugarcane. Because of the popularity of the railroad as a means of transportation, kids were taught where the primary railroads of the United States were located. Kids in the early 20th century learned all about gold, silver, iron, copper, aluminum, and coal mining. In fact, mining was so important that it was a major reason for the settlement and statehood of territories such as Nevada, California, and Alaska.

Vacation: Geography for Sale!

THESE DAYS, most Americans learn firsthand about US geography. With the invention of the automobile and then the airplane, travel for pleasure became much more common. Today, on the July 4 weekend alone, about 40 million Americans go on a road trip.

What are the reasons people go on vacation? One of the main reasons is to get a change of scen-

➤ Regular schoolbooks were not the only places where kids learned about geography. This map of the Holy Land is from an 1884 book used to teach Sunday School children about the Bible.

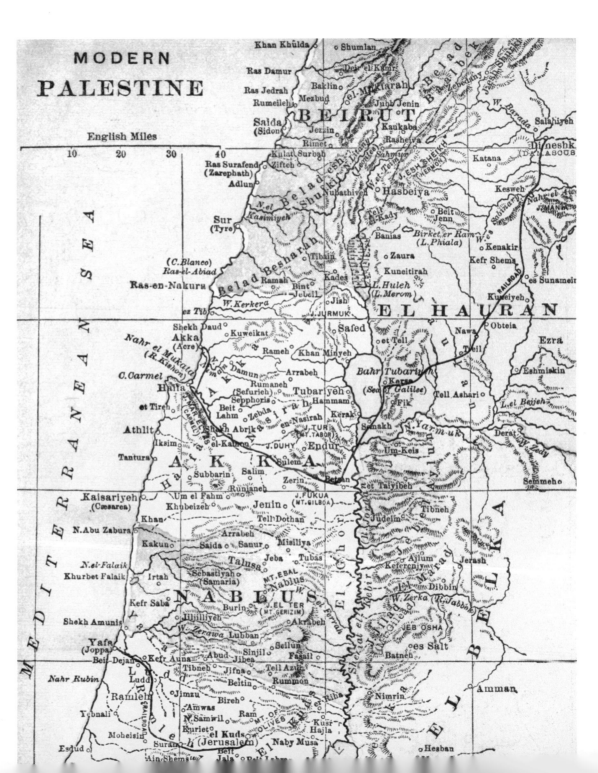

ery, or a change of geography. States and cities all around the country promote the uniqueness of their location, telling outsiders what makes Sheboygan, Wisconsin; or Reno, Nevada; or Portland, Oregon, interesting and special. The souvenirs vacationers buy, whether postcards, spoons, plates, or T-shirts, are reminders of the unique geography of the different and exciting places they visited.

Railroads and the Expanding Country

AFTER THE first operating railroad began in 1828, the rapid spread of train routes farther and farther west led to a great deal of survey and mapping work. Each railroad company needed to survey the land through which its rails would run and then determine the best path for the tracks. Railroads also played a major role in the development of towns along their routes, since the federal government provided land grants of strips of land, called *right-of-way*, along the tracks for each mile of railroad tracks laid. In many cases the railroads actually owned the land upon which towns were built.

Maps of the United States began to include railroad routes. When new railroad routes were created, maps fell out of date and new ones were printed. Railroad maps were very important because they helped people find the best way to get to their destination, the way road maps do today, and also helped merchants plan shipments of their goods. By 1850 there were just over 8,500 miles of railroad in operation in the country, going only as far west as Kentucky, Wisconsin, and Indiana. Ultimately, the various railroad companies received more than 94 million acres of land from the government.

Because railroad engines cannot pull railcars up slopes of more than a few degrees, railroad tracks must be laid on flat or nearly flat ground, and the American geography had to be altered to accommodate them. Hilly ground was leveled wherever possible.

The biggest obstacle to expanding westward during the early years of the American railroad was crossing the Allegheny Mountains. In 1854, a 3,612-foot-long tunnel, 24 feet wide and 21 feet high, was bored through a mountainside for the Pennsylvania Railroad at a cost of nearly $500,000, a tremendous sum in those days. Another large tunnel was built during the mid-19th century for the Blue Ridge Railroad, crossing the Blue Ridge Mountains in Virginia. It was 4,273 feet long and also cost about $500,000.

By 1860, the eastern half of the United States was completely crisscrossed with train tracks, and railroad companies were beginning to go farther west. At this point there were 30,000 miles of railroad tracks around the nation.

The Homestead Act of 1862 was a major force in the rapid settling of the American West. The act proclaimed that heads of families could obtain

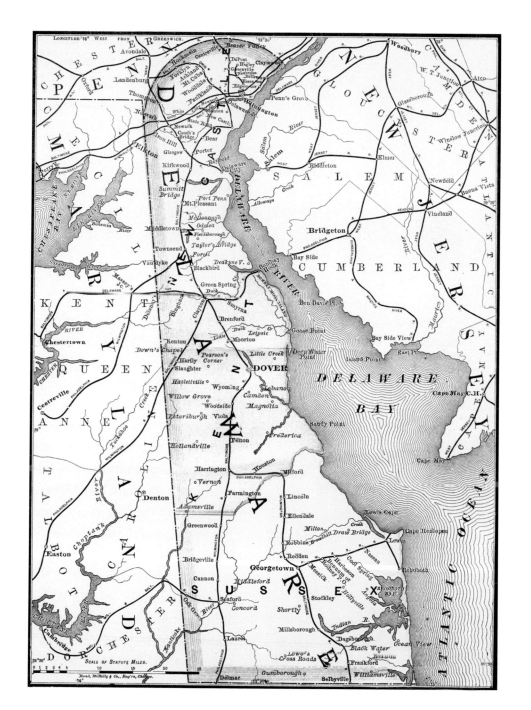

➤ This 19th century map of Delaware shows details of all the rail lines and stations. Roads existed, but until the invention of the automobile, railroads were much more important to show on maps.

as many as 160 acres of land for free, with just a 10-dollar fee for the transaction and a two-dollar fee for the land agent. More than one million acres of land were granted under this legislation by the end of the Civil War. The Pacific Railway Act of 1862 made it a priority to develop a continuous railway link from Nebraska to San Francisco. By 1870, there were nearly 53,000 miles of track in operation, and by 1900, there were almost 200,000 miles of track laid.

These days, when we think of rail travel around the United States, most of us think only of one name: Amtrak. But that was not the case in the 19th century. In 1874, there were 500 different railroad companies in the United States, from A (the Adirondack) to W (the Worcester and Somerset). So it was not enough for railroad maps just to show routes; each route was usually labeled with the name of the company operating the line. Each railroad company had its own timetables and route maps, and advertised key features of its rail line. For example, the Philadelphia, Wilmington and Baltimore Railroad advertised that it had a route to New Orleans that was 221 miles shorter than any other from the north.

Theodore Roosevelt

DURING THE 19th century, increasing industrialization and rapid settlement of the western frontier changed the geography of the United States, placing towns, factories, and railroads in places that had previously been wilderness. Theodore Roosevelt was the first president to really have a finer appreciation of the nation's geography, its resources, and its geological splendor. Long before he became president, he spent a lot of time exploring the West and writing about its wonders from his ranch in the Dakota Territory.

Roosevelt knew that the nation's natural resources were limited and had to be protected. As president, he was a major force behind the passage of the Reclamation Act of 1902, which called for irrigation of dry land in the West. He was also concerned with protecting the country's forests. He helped create the US Forest Service in 1905, and during his time in office the country gained 151 million acres of national forests. Roosevelt created the Inland Waterways Commission in 1907 and the National Conservation Commission in 1908 to take stock of the nation's natural resources. He also oversaw the creation of several national parks: Crater Lake, Oregon; Wind Cave, South Dakota; Platt, Oklahoma; Sully Hill, North Dakota; and Mesa Verde, Colorado. During his presidency, the Antiquities Act was also passed, which permitted presidents to protect natural wonders on government land from development.

At the laying of the cornerstone of the gateway to Yellowstone National Park in Gardiner, Montana, on April 24, 1903, Roosevelt said:

The Yellowstone Park is something absolutely unique in the world, so far as I know. Nowhere else in any civilized country is there to be found such a tract of veritable wonderland made accessible to all visitors. . . .

The geysers, the extraordinary hot springs, the lakes, the mountains, the canyons, and cataracts unite to make this region something not wholly to be paralleled elsewhere on the globe. It must be kept for the benefit and enjoyment of all of us; and I hope to see a steadily increasing number of our people take advantage of its attractions. At present it is rather singular that a greater number of people come from Europe to see it than come from our own Eastern States. The people near by seem awake to its beauties; and I hope that more and more of our people who dwell far off will appreciate its really marvelous character. . . .

The preservation of the forests is of course the matter of prime importance in every public reserve of this character. In this region of the Rocky Mountains and the great plains the problem of the water supply is the most important which the home-maker has to face. Congress has not of recent years done anything wiser than in passing the irrigation bill; and nothing is more essential to the preservation of the water supply than the preservation of the forests.

The US Geological Survey

EARLY ON, the government recognized the usefulness of geographers to the nation. During the Revolutionary War, Congress authorized the hiring of several well-paid geographers for use by the US Army. During the War of 1812, Congress authorized the appointment of eight topographic engineers and eight assistant topographic engineers, part of the first Corps of Topographic Engineers in the army, and that corps continued to function as a unit until it was incorporated into the Corps of Engineers in 1863 (during the Civil War). Between the Louisiana Purchase in 1803 and 1861, more than 100 exploring and mapping expeditions were sent west of the Mississippi River by the War Department to explore natural resources and find routes for wagon roads to the Pacific Coast.

On March 3, 1849, Congress passed a bill authorizing the creation of a Department of the Interior. Among the original duties of the new department was exploration of the west, management of public parks, oversight of Native American and public lands, and the administration of

patents. Beginning in 1850, the Department's Mexican Boundary Commission began work to set the international boundary with Mexico. The department began to do a geological survey of the western territories in 1869.

In 1872, Congress voted to make Yellowstone the country's first national park. Seven years later, in 1879, it created the US Geological Survey (USGS) within the Department of the Interior, requiring it to perform "classification of the public lands, and examination of the geological structure, mineral resources, and products of the national domain." In 1882, the USGS began carefully mapping the topography of the United States.

The earliest government maps were created mainly for miners, farmers, timber producers, and engineers. The work of the USGS in 1884–85 included activities all across the United States. Four parties were put in the field to survey the topography of New England. Six topographic parties and two triangulation parties entered the field to survey the Appalachian region. Geology was studied in parts of Virginia and Maryland. Two parties were sent into Arizona, and work was also started in Texas, Kansas, Missouri, and Arkansas. Special topographic and geological surveys were taken in Yellowstone National Park. An ongoing survey of glacial formations in the

➢ A War Department map of the area surrounding the Yellowstone and Missouri Rivers, 1859–60.

Rocky Mountains continued, as did geological work in Michigan, Wisconsin, and Minnesota. The extinct volcanoes of the Rocky Mountain and Cascade ranges were also studied, the coal lands of the Great Sioux reservation in Dakota were examined, and work continued on the geological exploration of the cinnabar (red mineral) deposits of California.

Topographic mapping of the entire country was a huge undertaking. By 1924, more than 40 years after the project began, only 40 percent of the country had been mapped by the USGS.

Today, the topographic mapping of the nation is complete, and you can obtain a topo map (as it is called, for short) of any corner of the United States. Nevertheless, the work of the USGS is expansive and ongoing.

Nautical Charts

PEOPLE USE maps to help find where they are in relation to certain reference points on land. When there are no reference points, a map is pretty much

➤ The explorer and scientist John Wesley Powell's survey party ready to start its work for the Department of Interior in Sweetwater County, Wyoming, May 1871.

useless. Imagine you are a ship's captain sailing across the Atlantic Ocean. Would a detailed map of the ocean help you? What details would it reveal? There would not be any details, since there are no landmarks or reference points in the middle of the ocean.

On the other hand, once a ship approaches a coastline, a map becomes very important. Coastal maps are known as charts—nautical charts, marine charts, naval charts, coastal charts, and harbor charts.

These charts have been around for hundreds of years, and their accuracy has improved greatly over time. Modern-day nautical charts contain a lot of information, all of it vital for navigating a bay, harbor, estuary, or other water body bordering land. Boaters need to know the water depths, tides, and currents. They need to know the location of rocks, buoys, wrecks, reefs, sandbars, islands, and other danger spots to avoid when navigating near land. Throughout history, thousands of lives and billions of dollars' worth of merchandise have been lost due to shipwrecks.

The US Coast and Geodetic Survey (USC&GS) is charged with surveying the coasts, harbors, and tidal estuaries of the United States. Established in 1807 by President Thomas Jefferson, it was originally called the Survey of the Coast. Its mission, which has not changed in over 200 years, is to survey the US coastline and create nautical charts. The first official US hydrographic survey was conducted in 1834, and in 1839 the federal government issued its very first nautical chart. The earliest methods of hydrographic survey were the sounding pole (simply a long pole with depth markings) and the lead line (lead-weighted ropes with depth markings). Both were done manually.

In 1878, the agency was renamed the US Coast and Geodetic Survey, and in 1970, the agency became a part of the newly created National Oceanic and Atmospheric Administration (NOAA) under its National Ocean Service (NOS) branch. Modern depth measurements are taken through sounding methods, such as sonar. While coastal soundings are very complete, details of the vast oceans' seafloor topography are not complete yet. Existing images are created from data from satellites, shipboard depth soundings, and any actual underwater seafloor exploration (which has been limited). A manned bathyscaphe (a specially designed underwater vehicle able to withstand the high pressure of the deep sea) named the *Trieste* went to a depth of 35,802 feet in the deepest part of the Pacific Ocean in 1960.

Nautical charts are packed with useful information that can help prevent shipwrecks. The chart on the next page shows Boston Harbor. As you can see, depth soundings are fewer and farther between in open waters and more frequent the closer one gets to land. The dashed lines on the chart represent underwater topographic features. Water depths can change greatly over a short distance, so it is important for navigators to know where the shoals (shallows) are located. Depths also change over time, so charts must be updated every so often. Especially in harbors, rivers, and anywhere near land, sediment can build up as dirt-carrying storm water is emptied into the water and as erosion occurs. Dredging, the mechanical removal of sediment, is often necessary to make coastal waters navigable. Unless the causes of the sediment buildup are eliminated, dredging is likely to be needed again, and it is common in major harbors.

Besides water depths, navigators need to know the strength and direction of currents. In the chart of Boston Harbor, the currents are shown by the red lines and arrows. As with any map or chart, the particular features are a kind of code and have to be deciphered. In this case, the lines show the direction and speed of the currents when they are at their maximum velocity. The arrow indicates direction of the current, and the letter and numbers are a code telling ships' crews when the current reaches its maximum velocity. So L + 257 means that the current reaches its peak speed 2 hours and 57 minutes after the low tide (in this case the low tide at the Boston Navy Yard). An H + 257 at the other end of the same arrow would mean that 2 hours and 57 minutes after the high tide, the ebb current has its

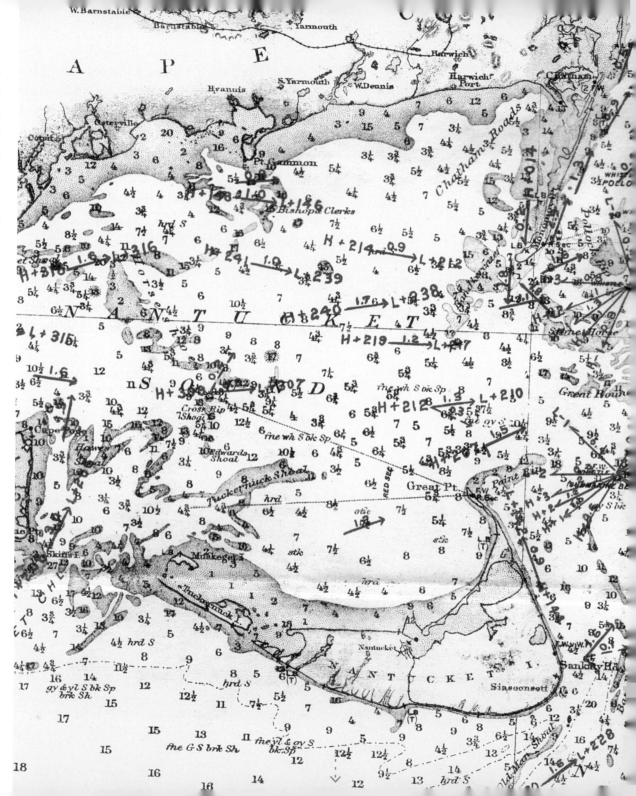

➤ Chart of Boston Harbor, 1911.

greatest velocity in the opposite direction. Another useful tool on many sea charts is a detailed picture of a compass, so that navigators can carefully check their bearing, or position.

The chart also uses abbreviations to give details about the kind of material on the harbor floor. So *crs yl & wh S blk Sp brk Sh* means "coarse yellow and white sand, with black specks and broken shells," while *gn M* means "green mud." Why do you suppose a ship's captain would need to know this information?

The chart was accompanied by extensive written directions. For example, approaching Boston Harbor from Cape Cod,

Vessels standing for Boston light will cross the southwesterly end of Stellwagen Bank, *in depths of 12 to 15 fathoms; this bank, with depths of less than 20 fathoms on it, begins 5 miles northward of the north end of Cape Cod and extends in a northerly direction for 17½ miles, its width varying from 8 miles at its southerly end to about 2 miles near its northerly end. Soundings on the Stellwagen Bank cannot be depended on to locate a position on the bank except in the case of soundings in a depth of 9½ fathoms, the shoalest water, which is found near its extreme southwest end. The prevailing depths over the shoaler parts of the bank are 12 to 15 fathoms.*

The latest government nautical charts are updated weekly and available on a print-on-demand basis through the Office of Coastal Survey (OCS) website. Besides sediment buildup and dredging, there are other reasons to constantly update the charts. New buoys or lights are sometimes installed or old ones removed; new shipwrecks or other obstructions are located; and new docking facilities are constructed. The OCS currently offers five types of charts: harbor charts (for navigation and anchorage in small harbors and waterways), coast charts (for navigation inside offshore reefs and shoals and entering bays and harbors), general charts (for use by offshore vessels), sailing charts (charts showing information for approaching the coast from the open ocean), and small-craft charts (with special information

WATCH FOR THE BUSHY TREE

The first American book of American sailing directions was the *American Coastal Pilot*, published in 1796 by Edmund Blunt. The directions for sailing into Portland, Maine, were somewhat vague:

In steering the above course you may see a round bushy tree to the northwest of the town, and a house with one chimney. You bring the tree to the northwest of the house, which course will bring you up the channel way in 6 or 7 fathoms waters; but when you come abreast of the fort which stands on a hill you haul away W.S.W. for there is a shoal bank on your starboard hand.

for small boats). The OCS has five series of charts: Atlantic, Pacific, Alaska, Great Lakes, and Gulf Coast. To keep its charts accurate, the OCS partners with many other agencies.

➤ An 1858 chart of Milford Haven and Pembroke, in Western Wales, Great Britain. The government commissioned these official "admiralty surveys." In 1897, for example, 11 ships carrying 831 men were sent on hydrography missions around the British Empire.

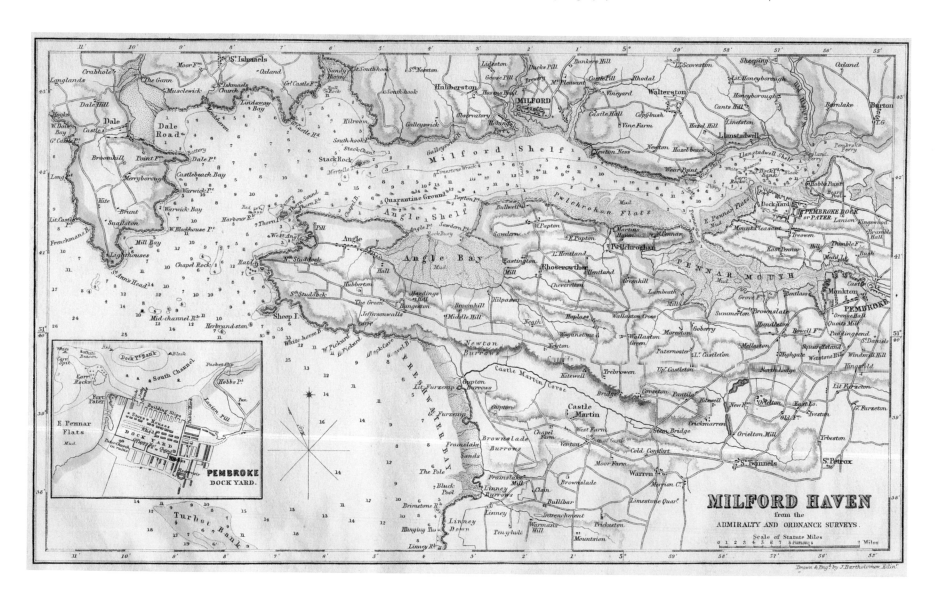

MAKE A NAUTICAL CHART

JUST as maps show topography (the contours of the surface), sea charts show the depth of water (that is, the contours of the seafloor, or underwater topography). This information is extremely useful to anyone who is trying to navigate a boat. Through the ages, thousands of shipwrecks have been caused by reefs, shoals, and rocks.

You'll Need
➤ Shovel
➤ Handful of rocks, various sizes
➤ Bucket(s) of water
➤ 4 dowels, about 12 inches long each
➤ Yardstick (or tape measure)
➤ String, at least 50 feet
➤ Scissors
➤ 45/45/90 drafting triangle (or a square piece of cardboard)
➤ Graph paper
➤ Pencil
➤ 2 12-inch rulers
➤ Calculator

Find a place outdoors where you can dig a hole, about a foot long by 8 inches wide. Do not make the hole one uniform depth. For example, you can make it shallow (2 inches) around the edges, but deeper (6 or more inches) as you go toward the center. Or you could make it mostly shallow but with a few deep trenches in spots.

When you are done digging, pat the bottom of the hole with your palms to compact the dirt as much as possible. Put the two largest rocks aside.

Scatter the rest of the rocks in the hole, especially in the shallow areas.

Get a bucket (or buckets) of water and very slowly fill the hole. The sides may erode a little as you pour, but that's okay. Stop when you are about a half inch or so from the ground surface.

Next, make a grid so you can take and record depth measurements on your chart. To do this, first place a dowel into the ground near each of the corners of the pond. The distance between the dowels along the longer sides of the pond should be 14 inches and along the shorter sides, 12 inches. Tie a string from one dowel to the next (at about 6

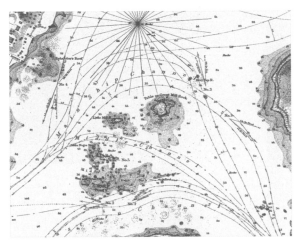

➤ An 1851 chart of Hell Gate, New York. Hell Gate, as the name implies, had dangerous reefs that had to be avoided. The same year this chart was published, the US Army began to blast away some of the dangerous rocks that had long been the enemy of ship's captains.

inches above the ground level) and use the drafting triangle to make sure you have a perfect rectangle (adjust the dowels if necessary). Your chart's scale will be 1:2, so on your graph paper, draw a rectangle that is 7 by 6 inches.

Cut 7 pieces of string that are each 18 inches long, and 5 pieces of string that are each 22 inches long. Tie pieces of string from one side of the rectangle to the other at 1-inch intervals, so when you are done you have a grid of strings, as shown.

Lightly duplicate this grid on your graph paper. Since your scale is 1:2, the grid lines should be 1 inch apart on the paper. Now, with a ruler, and at each of the intersections of the grid that fall above the "pond," measure the depth down to the nearest 16th of an inch. Use your calculator to figure out the decimal value. (Example: 4³⁄₁₆ would be 4.19 inches.)

Record each depth number at the correct point on your chart.

Bird's-Eye Views

DURING THE mid-19th century, a new type of map became popular. Called the *bird's-eye view,* this map was a three-dimensional look at a town or city as if seen from the point of view of a bird hundreds or thousands of feet in the sky flying toward the settlement. Bird's-eye view lithographs were the precursors of aerial photographs, but bird's-eye views were drawn by hand using detailed information about the place in question, and were shown at an angle, as if the bird were approaching the town, not looking down on it from directly overhead.

Because of the angle at which they were shown, these views could not be used for navigational purposes; they were just meant to be interesting, flattering portraits of the growth of the nation. Their purpose was to show how a particular town was prospering, which could be determined by the number of smokestacks and church steeples, among other things.

➤ A bird's-eye view of Virginia City, Nevada, in 1875. Some of the towns shown in bird's-eye views experienced sudden, rapid growth due to gold and silver mining activities but then lost population as the precious metals were depleted. In 1880, the population of Virginia City was nearly 11,000. By 1940, the population was only 500.

The Western towns shown in these views were sometimes set against rugged and wild backdrops. The neat grid of the town set against these wide, open spaces showed how people could conquer geography and tame the environment.

➤ This is a bird's-eye view of the just-founded town of Hailey in the Wood River Valley, Idaho, in 1884.

Automobiles, Highways, and the Road Map

As DIFFERENT modes of transportation became popular, settlement patterns changed. When ships and boats were the primary means of transporting goods around the country, towns and cities were most commonly built along the coast,

or along rivers or lakes with connections to rivers. With the birth of the railroad, towns sprang up along train routes. Places that were not along the railroad route were inconvenient because they could only be reached by horse and carriage.

Just like the railroad before it, the invention of the automobile during the late 19th century changed the way Americans thought about the geography of their country. It did not happen immediately, however. The cars of the late 1890s were expensive, could go only a few miles per hour, and had no tops or windshields to protect against bad weather, so their owners could not drive them very far. Within a few years, many improvements were made to cars, prices fell, and the number of autos on American roads increased dramatically.

In 1900, there were only 8,000 registered automobiles in the entire United States. By 1905, the number had increased to 77,000, and by 1910 it was 458,000. By the time Henry Ford introduced the affordable Model T in 1910s, cars could reach a top speed of about 40 miles per hour. By 1915, two million cars were registered in the United States.

Outside of the cities, the roads that existed during the early years of the 20th century were mainly dusty, unpaved, and narrow. They had been laid out for horse and carriage, which made early drivers adventurers. They wore caps and goggles to protect their hair and eyes from the wind. They also needed maps to help them get where they were going. No longer did they rely on others (train engineers or stagecoach drivers) to take them places. Automobile drivers now had to navigate their own way over hundreds of miles.

The earliest forms of automobile maps were very interesting. They were called *photo-auto maps* because they featured detailed directions combined with photographs of all the key places along a certain route, such as turnoffs, forks in the road, or major landmarks—buildings, large trees, boulders, and so on. Because early road signs were poor and some roads were very winding and confusing, these maps were the best way to show a driver that he was going the right direction. He knew that if he did not pass the large tree or that old factory shown in the photo, he had made a wrong turn. The photos were black and white, and the maps were low-quality, so they may not have been that useful. Of course, this type of map had a limited usefulness anyway, because it became outdated so fast. The landscape changed when buildings were knocked down and others were built, and as new roads were created and old ones changed. Someone with a photo-auto map that was a year or two old might easily get lost.

As the number of cars increased, so did the number and quality of roads. One of the earliest and most legendary highways was Route 66. Originally begun in 1926, the road stretched over 2,400 miles from Chicago, Illinois, to Los Angeles, California, passing through Missouri, Kansas,

21.8 Cross dangerous bridge over the railroad.

21.9 At the second road, at Johren's Hotel, turn left.
22.0 Just beyond railroad crossing. Crossing not protected by gates.

24.4 At a cross roads turn left.
24.7 Cross bridge over the railroad.

Oklahoma, Texas, New Mexico, and Arizona along the way.

By 1930, there were 23 million registered cars. More and more roads were being built as cars became the favorite mode of transportation. New roads were built in varying sizes and types: turnpikes (toll roads), parkways, highways, and expressways. They differed from one another in their width and purpose. Some cut through cities, while others crossed rural areas.

This network of roads grew as quickly as the network of railroad tracks had during the middle of the 19th century. And just as the railroad had done more than half a century earlier, highways brought prosperity to the areas they crossed through. Shops, restaurants, and motels sprang up along highways. With the advent of cars, gas stations were also a common roadside sight.

Suddenly, people who had never left their hometowns before were traveling around the nation, visiting new and exciting places for the first time. Highways helped travelers access their country by cutting through difficult terrain such as mountains, deserts, and swamps.

The increasing popularity of automobiles also led to a new phenomenon in cartography: the road map. Unlike the photo-auto maps, road maps did

> LEFT: Photo-auto map showing how to reach the Vanderbilt Cup Race, Long Island, New York, in 1904. *Courtesy of Historical Society of Westburys*

CREATE A PHOTO-AUTO MAP

PHOTO-AUTO maps were a combination of spelled-out directions, simple map sketches, and photographs of key landmarks and intersections. For example, in the program for the 1906 Vanderbilt Cup Race on Long Island, a photo-auto map was shown to tell drivers how to get to the race from New York City. Interestingly, though these maps have not been produced for many decades, modern technology now allows us the option to "see" the landmarks along our route using detailed satellite photography or Google's Street View—proving that maybe our ancestors were on to something when they created photo-auto maps.

You'll Need
➤ Digital camera
➤ Notebook
➤ Pen
➤ 2 friends
➤ Computer

Figure out a route in your neighborhood, between a half mile and one mile long, for which you'd like to create a photo-auto map. It is best to find a route that contains several different streets and some twists and turns.

Bring your camera, notebook, pen, and a friend with you on a walk around your neighborhood. (Or, you can ask an adult to drive you.) Your goal is to create accurate directions using about 10 to 15 photos.

Make sure you have one photo of the starting point and one of the ending point. Choose some key landmarks along the way that would help someone determine they are going the right way. Take notes to go along with each photo you take; for example, "Continue until you reach an intersection, where you'll see a large house with a For Sale sign on the lawn." And remember, since road signs were often lacking in the old days, don't always give the name of the road; the goal is to try to give directions using landmarks and other notable points along the route. Take about double the number of photos you will need so later you can select only the best from the bunch.

When you get home, upload the digital photos to your computer. Type up your notes and insert a photo to go along with each set of directions—one photo per page. Use the image tool in your word processor to change the photo to black and white. When you are done, you should have a 10- to 15-page photo-auto map.

Now, to test how well you did, give this map to another friend or a family member and see if he or she can follow along and get to the ending point.

Just after passing through a double row of willows, cross the railroad.

➤ Photo-auto map image from 1906. *Courtesy of Historical Society of Westburys*

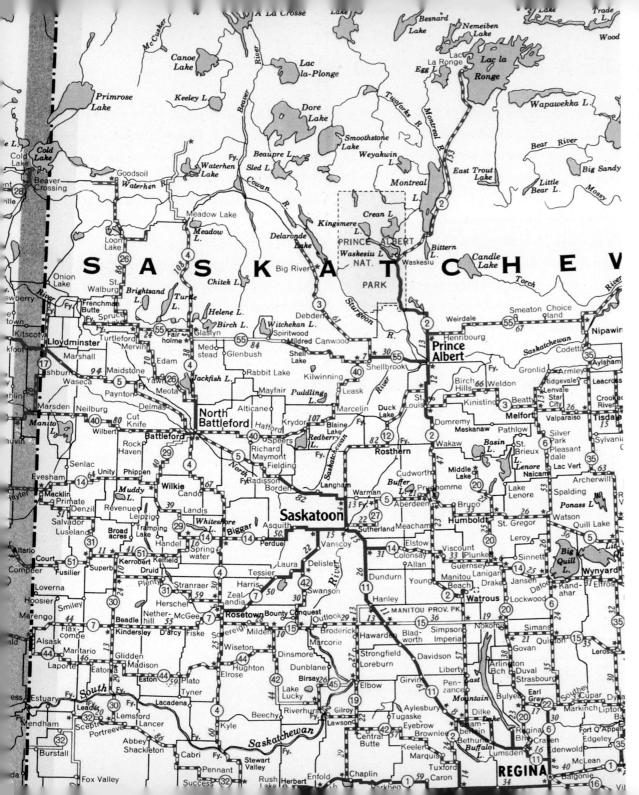

not focus on one particular route. Rather, they were created for navigation around entire states, or even regions of the country (New England, for example). They relied upon better highway and road names and signs.

These unique creations were foldable and designed to be convenient for the automobile traveler. They could be stored in a car's glove compartment or door pocket. Armed with these maps, drivers could now navigate their way across the country. No longer were rail lines shown in detail on all maps; this was not something drivers needed to see. Now, it was highways that crisscrossed the maps, cutting routes that were sometimes even more direct than rail lines. Trips that once took days by horse and carriage could now be accomplished in less than a day, and sometimes in a matter of a few hours.

Understanding geography was more important than ever as Americans took to the road more often. To encourage people to drive, gas stations often issued road maps to their customers, and state governments gave them away for free to encourage tourism.

By the 1950s, when there were 50 million registered automobiles in the country, infrastructure had improved greatly. Old dirt roads were widened

➤ A 1953 Canadian road map. The red/white colored lines indicate gravel roads, while the solid red lines show paved roads.

and paved, and many thousands of miles of new highways were built. Symbols distinguish the different types of highways: interstate highways, US highways, state highways, and county highways, including freeways, highways, parkways, and toll roads. As more Americans bought cars, more of them took to the roads for both business and pleasure. Road maps became a necessity and could be found in every car's glove compartment. Road atlases, featuring road maps of all 50 states, were popular with people making cross-country trips.

State Shapes

SOME STATES are fairly uniform in their shapes or geographical features, while others are very unique. Maryland is an example of the latter. Close to the ocean, it has coastal plains and many marshes and wetlands. Farther inland it has a hillier Piedmont Plateau, and still farther west it has a mountainous region.

Each area has its own distinct vegetation and industries. The plateau is ideal for farming, while the mountainous region has been used for mining. Maryland's shape is also unique. At its most narrow point the state is only two miles wide, and at its widest point it is still only 124 miles from northern to southern border.

The shapes of our states sometimes create interesting boundaries. One of the most interest-

ROUTE 66

Route 66 was fully paved by 1938 and reached its peak of popularity in the 1940s and 1950s. A song called "(Get Your Kicks on) Route 66" was composed in 1946 and later recorded by artists such as Nat King Cole, Chuck Berry, and the Rolling Stones.

However, after President Eisenhower signed the Interstate Highway Act in the 1950s, new, wider interstate highways were built near Route 66, eventually making it obsolete. The once busy Route 66 was officially abandoned in 1985. Today only pieces of the famous road remain intact.

➤ Historic Route 66 Motel sign, Kingman, Arizona.

ing geographical points in the country is the Four Corners, the only spot in the country where four states meet (New Mexico, Arizona, Colorado, and Utah). This point is off US Route 160, on Four Corners Road, in the midst of two Indian reservations. Four Corners is very remote; the nearest community is six miles away. There has been a monument marking the spot since 1875, but it is actually 1,800 feet from the location for which it was intended. But, according to the government, once a border monument has been established and accepted, it marks the border, whether or not it was originally intended for that spot.

STUDY STATE SHAPES

THE shapes and sizes of states in the United States vary greatly. Some states are very regular in their shapes (Wyoming), while others are highly irregular (Maryland). In this activity, you will make a chart to study the most common types of state borders.

YOU'LL NEED
➤ Detailed map of the United States (an atlas with a detailed map of each individual state is best)
➤ Pad of graph paper or computer spreadsheet program
➤ Pen or pencil

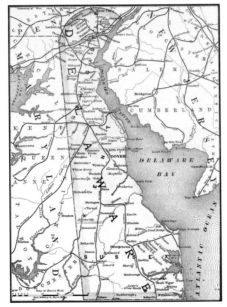

For each state, chart the number of each type of border. An *arbitrary border* is just a straight line. A *latitude/longitude border* is one that falls completely or partly on an exact parallel of latitude or longitude. A *river/lake border* is a border that entirely or partially follows a river or lake. A *coastal border* is along the Atlantic Ocean (or adjacent bay), Pacific Ocean, or Gulf of Mexico. On your graph paper, make one row for each of the 50 states, and make columns labeled with the titles in bold above. Count each distinct side or face of a state separately. If one border is partly arbitrary but partly follows a river, count it as river. Example:

South Dakota: three sides arbitrary, one side river

North Dakota: two sides arbitrary, one side latitude, one side river

New Jersey: one side arbitrary, one side river, two sides ocean

When you are done, total the numbers for each column (border type). What does the result tell you about the way state shapes were determined?

For the most part, state borders are logical. However, there are a few places where state borders seem to be inconsistent. The best known of these may be the "Southwick Jog" between Connecticut and Massachusetts. In 1642, the Massachusetts colony hired two surveyors, Nathaniel Woodward and Solomon Saffrey, to set the boundary between the two colonies. They were supposed to set the border line by measuring due west at a latitude "from a point three miles south of the most south-

WEST VIRGINIA

West Virginia is a unique state in more than one way. First, it has the highest average elevation of any state east of the Mississippi River. The second reason it is unique is due to its interesting shape and location. West Virginia is said to be the northernmost southern state (part of it is farther north than Pittsburgh, Pennsylvania, or Trenton, New Jersey), the southernmost northern state (part of it is farther south than Richmond, Virginia, and Lexington, Kentucky), the easternmost western state (part of it is as far east as Rochester, New York), and the westernmost eastern state (part of it is farther west than Columbus, Ohio).

erly branch of the Charles River." But their work was sloppy, and their line was several miles too far south. Connecticut disputed the survey.

In 1695, a new survey revealed the mistake. Massachusetts, however, refused to accept the results of the new survey. Proposals and counter-proposals were made over the years, but it was not until 1713 that an acceptable proposal was made. However, the new border line was north of the towns of Enfield, Suffield, and Woodstock, which were originally Massachusetts settlements. The two sides agreed to let Massachusetts retain control of those towns. However, the citizens of the towns were unhappy about being under Massachusetts's jurisdiction and asked in 1724 that their towns be admitted into Connecticut. In 1749, Connecticut voted to accept them, against Massachusetts's wishes.

It was not until 1804 that the whole dispute was resolved. As a concession to Massachusetts, Connecticut agreed to give up a two-and-a-half-square-mile piece of land at Southwick.

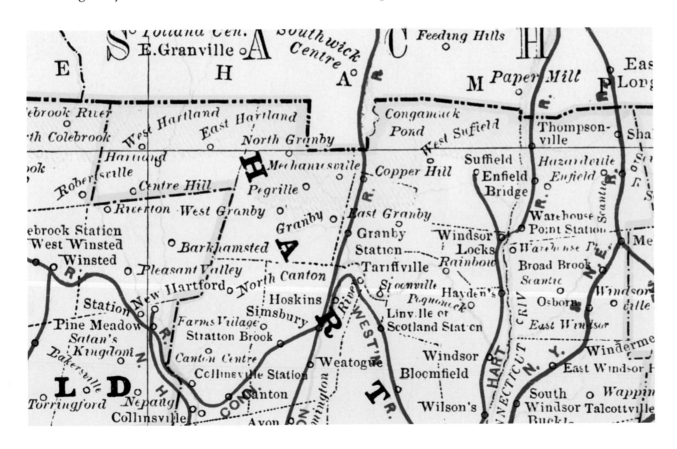

➤ The Southwick Jog, shown on an 1887 map of Connecticut.

MAP OF THE
GOLD REGIONS
OF
CALIFORNIA

Compiled from Original Surveys

BY JAMES WYLD.

Geographer to the Queen & Prince Albert

Charing Cross East & 2 Royal Exchange

Blood, Power, and Treasure:
Special Uses of Maps

Sometimes, geographical knowledge is the difference between life and death, wealth and poverty, or power and weakness. Maps can be fascinating and have long captured people's imagination. Unlocking the secrets of geography can help reveal enemy camps, lead the way to gold mines, and help seal political victory, among other things.

Geography and Warfare

➤ Plan of the city and citadel of Cambray, France, around 1700. Fortifications have long been used to protect against enemies. In this case, most of the city is surrounded by the citadel, a large, fortified wall.

THE OUTCOMES of battles are not just determined by the size and strength of the armies. They are often determined by the unique geographical features of the countries or territories in which the battles are fought. Transportation routes, which are laid out based on geographical features and obstacles, are vital to defending and invading armies. Existing roads and railroad tracks can be used successfully by invaders as paths for supplying their troops with food, supplies, and weapons.

The greater the natural barriers or obstacles—mountains, rivers, lakes, deserts, and coastlines—the better a country can resist invasion. Barriers give the defenders a chance to watch an invading army from a distance and prepare. Bridges over rivers can be intentionally destroyed to make it more difficult for the invaders to cross. Geographical areas that have limited access points give the defenders an advantage. Troops trying to come through a narrow mountain pass can be ambushed, or the way can be blockaded or booby-trapped.

The legendary military leaders of history share something in common: their ability to venture into new, foreign lands far from home. Hannibal, Alexander the Great, Attila the Hun, and Napoleon are all leaders who braved geographical obstacles to conquer others.

Geography plays a role not only on land but also at sea. An attacking fleet must have accurate naval charts and

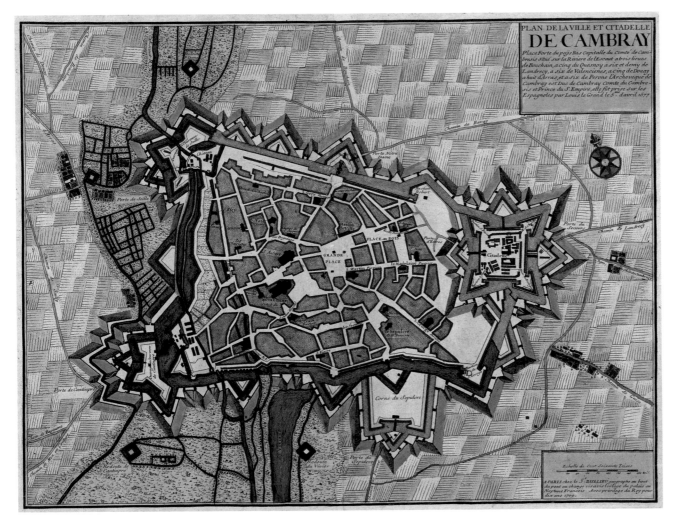

PLAN DE LA VILLE ET CITADELLE
DE CAMBRAY

know the location of any mines, icebergs, rocks, reefs, sandbars, and islands, as well as ocean depths and currents.

A defending country should know its own land better than the enemy does, including the best vantage points from which to spy on the enemy, the best defensive positions, and the best places to which to retreat. Of course, the invaders have probably studied the terrain very carefully, using the best available maps and firsthand information. Officers from both invading and defending armies alike would be likely to use the maps, along with details of previous battles, to find geographical weaknesses and strengths.

Some countries, such as Great Britain, have excellent natural defenses. As an island, Britain is protected by water on all sides. Since the Norman invasion of 1066, the island has not successfully been conquered. Even the powerful Nazi army did not attempt a direct invasion of Britain during World War II, choosing instead to bomb London from the air. Ships coming across the English Channel or arriving via the ocean can be spotted when they are still some distance away, and can be fired upon from the mainland.

Other countries, such as France, are not so lucky. France has suffered through more than a thousand years of invasions, beginning with the Roman era, when Franks and Burgundians entered.

At first glance, France seems to be well protected against invasion. It has several boundaries: the English Channel, the Atlantic Ocean, the Mediterranean Sea, and the Alps. There are also eight upland belts (bands of ridges) between Paris and the German border to the east. The west side of these ridges offers gentle slopes for the defenders, while the eastern side is steep, posing challenges

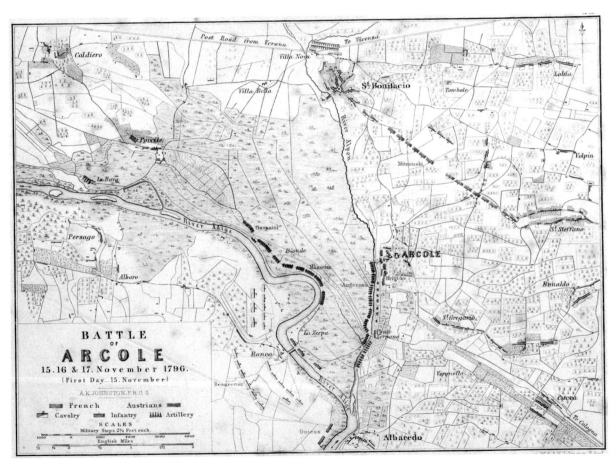

➤ This period map illustrates troop strength and positions during the three-day Battle of Arcole (1796) in Italy, between French forces led by Napoleon Bonaparte and Austrian forces led by Jozsef Alvinczi. The French forces are indicated in blue and the Austrians in yellow. The French won the battle.

for attackers. Nonetheless, when German forces invaded France in 1870, their large numbers and rapid mobilization allowed them to overcome this geographical obstacle.

The Germans were able to penetrate into France twice more, during World War I (1914–18) and again during World War II (1939–45), when they first occupied Belgium, Holland, and Luxembourg, giving them an easy entry into France from the north.

Because the Germans had control over most of Western Europe during World War II, it was much more difficult for the Allied forces to plan an attack. The Allies knew that to defeat the Nazis, they had to somehow get their armies from Great Britain, where they had been gathering, onto occupied continental Europe.

Allied Command decided on a two-pronged approach. First, in 1943 they thought up a plan to reach Italy and points north through a landing on the island of Sicily. When that was successful, they planned an invasion of France via the English Channel. Their selection of the beach at Normandy was carefully thought out based upon the potential location and strength of enemy forces. The Germans had a formidable defense set up along the coast, but it was both the element of surprise and the sheer size and force of the Allied invasion on D-Day, June 6, 1944, that helped the Allies overpower the coastal defenses and make a successful entry into France.

The geography of warfare is not just a factor of a country's location and physical features. It also depends on how far the country has extended its empire around the world. Territories acquired through conquest can prove important during world conflicts. At the start of World War II, the British Empire consisted of land on all seven continents. In North America, Britain controlled Canada, and in South America, the British West Indies. In Africa, the British controlled several countries, including Sudan and South Africa, while in Asia it ruled over the Indian subcontinent. In addition, Britain controlled the entire continent of Australia, and even parts of Antarctica. France controlled French Guiana and some islands in the Caribbean, as well as much of North and West Africa, and Indo-China.

During World War II, critical battles were fought all around the globe, including in North Africa, in places that were part of the French and British Empires. The invading Germans were led by a general who was so crafty and able to fight on this unfamiliar ground that he earned the nickname the Desert Fox. Erwin Rommel (1891–1944) led the Afrika Korps and drove the British from Libya, and then continued to push into Egypt. Despite the harsh desert conditions, Rommel was able to adapt military strategies that made his Afrika Korps very hard to defeat.

In the case of global war, geographical strategies are critical. Leading up to World War II, Nazi leaders planned their step-by-step takeover of Europe with an overall goal in mind. Each piece of the puzzle was another step toward their total domination of continental Europe. Austria and Czechoslovakia to the south; Poland to the east; and Belgium, Luxembourg, and Holland to the west were all part of the strategy. Conquest of Poland was necessary, for example, for the Nazis to invade Russia. Allied forces led by the Americans were engaged in "island hopping," fighting one key battle after another with the goal of getting control of the South Pacific and operating closer to Japan, their target.

The size of the country or territory being invaded is always an important consideration. This is one thing that made the invasion of Russia in 1941 such a great challenge for the Germans. It is hard for any size army to infiltrate such a large country. The Germans needed great resources, and the remoteness of parts of Russia made it hard for the necessary supplies to reach the battlefront. Ultimately, the invasion of Russia helped cause the defeat of the Germans by diverting too many of their resources away from Western Europe, where the Allies were attacking.

During a war of such global proportions, the Allies had to find the best route for supplies to get to the battlefront. Thanks to new and faster airplanes, every place on earth was somehow affected by the war. After the attack on Pearl Harbor, military leaders had to be prepared for anything, even an invasion of the US mainland. Military

GEOGRAPHY IN WORLD WAR I

In 1918, a Harvard geology professor published a book called *A Handbook of Northern France* for American soldiers "who may wish to learn something of the leading physical features of the brave country where their aid will be so welcome." The author gave many examples of how geographical knowledge could be helpful during the fighting in France, including the places where trenches could easily be dug and the history of where the Germans had been successful, or not, in attacking.

Below are two firsthand accounts of fighting during World War I from soldiers' diaries. Notice how the terrain of the battlefield played a big part in combat.

Some of the most deadly contests of the war have been held in the forests of France. If you should ask me what feature of warfare was harder and fiercer than "going over the top" [of a hill] in the lot of an infantryman, there would be no hesitation in my reply—forest fighting. The Kaiser and his military advisers had put their infantry through the most thorough training in this secret and concealed method of fighting.

The Argonne Forest was a miniature Adirondack Mountains forest. It was about ten or twelve miles wide and about twenty-five miles deep. The [Germans] had held this ground for four years. They knew every foot of it and had every modern means of defense installed. At one point we encountered nine main line trenches, and one hundred or more minor systems. They had machine-guns set up in stages the leg height, the waist height, and shoulder height. That any troops could penetrate this forest of death was a marvel. More than 40,000 French troops were lost there . . . the German system of trenches and dugouts was so close-knit.

leaders looked for the geographical weak spots on the mainland and figured that from the East Coast, the enemy could invade by going up the Hudson-Mohawk Valley in New York, through the

WAR STRATEGY GAME

THE strategy of troop placement during ground wars has always been challenging. The best strategies involve planning ahead, not just action or reaction. Knowledge of geography is key to planning strategy.

In this activity, you will play an Allied general and use this vintage map of Eastern Europe to place your troops. The Axis enemy is trying to advance farther west, and it is your job to prevent the enemy from reaching its objective, the city of Huszth.

You'll Need
➤ Red pencil or marker
➤ Green pencil or marker
➤ Poster board (optional)
➤ Chess pieces (optional)

Make a photocopy of the map below. Each triangle represents 2,000 enemy troops. The current positions of your regiments (also 2,000 troops) are marked by squares. Study the current placement of enemy regiments. A regiment can move 30 miles in a day (or 10 miles through mountain passes).

Given the enemy's goal of Huszth, use the red pencil to try to predict the movement of the enemy over the next five days, marking each day's progress. Note that mountains can only be crossed through the passes shown on the map.

Plan your troop movements using the green pencil. Mark the final endpoints of both armies at the end of five days. Which side do you think has the advantage?

To do this activity with a friend, enlarge the photocopy, tape it to a poster board, and use chess pieces instead of the pencils to mark the troops' movements.

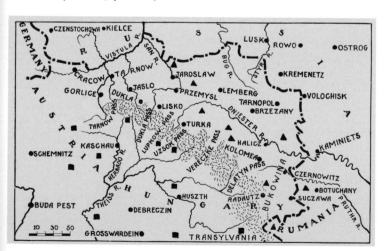

Chesapeake Bay and up the Susquehanna Valley in Pennsylvania, or through the Potomac Valley and Cumberland Gap in Maryland, Virginia, and West Virginia. From the southern coast, invaders could come through the Mississippi-Missouri Valley or through the mouth of the Colorado River in Mexico and push north along the Colorado and Gila Rivers in Arizona and California.

In a war, whether in ancient Greece, Civil War Virginia, or the modern-day Middle East, the best way to prepare is to thoroughly analyze all the geographical possibilities.

➤ Maps have also been used as means of propaganda during wars. During World War II, the Russians dropped booklets on German troops on the Eastern front. These booklets featured a map showing Latvia and western Russia, with text (in German so the German soldiers could read it) explaining how the Russians had successfully advanced farther west and were pushing back the German troops.

The Rapidly Changing World Map

WHILE THE physical geography of the world has not changed much in the last 200 years, the political geography has changed drastically. The reason mapmakers have remained in business over the years is that maps become outdated very quickly. Between 1800 and 1900, the map of the United States changed 29 times because of the addition of new states to the Union. Between 1810 and 1820 alone, the map changed seven times!

The US map is not the only one that changed often. The boundaries on the world map are constantly being redrawn. The most common reasons for changing national boundaries have been war, territorial expansion (colonialism), consolidation (the joining together of two or more countries into one), and dissolution (the splitting of a country into two or more smaller ones).

Though the countries of Italy, France, and Germany, for example, existed long ago, they were quite different from the unified modern countries we know today. Look at the map of France in 1361, following the Treaty of Bretigny. Not only did England have major possessions in France (shown in red), but there were more political divisions of the remaining land between the French crown and the King of Navarre.

➤ Map showing English possessions in France in 1361.

For example, your friend might say, "My ancestors came to this country from Germany in 1860," but the official unification of the German states did not occur until 1871. So the ancestors' immigration records would not name Germany as the place of origin, but rather Hesse, Saxony, or one of the others states that would later become part of official Germany.

Even then, after unification, the map of Germany would change. Look at the map on the next page of Germany in 1882. At that time, the powerful Kingdom of Prussia, colored in pink, extended all the way into Poland. Since its formation in 1701, Prussia had gained strength and size because it absorbed various German states, or added them through warfare.

However, the 1882 map of Germany would not remain valid for long. Over the next several decades, there were major changes. After Germany's loss in World War I, Prussian Kaiser Wilhelm II abdicated his throne and the Kingdom of Prussia officially came to an end, though Prussia still existed in name as part of Germany. By the end of World War II in 1945, Germany was reduced to just a fraction of its former size, and much of the territory that Prussia had taken from Poland was returned.

Following World War II, the stability of the world map did not last for long. Major changes came to Africa in the mid-20th century with the end of the colonial era, and to Europe in the late 20th century with breakup of the Soviet Union and the Eastern Bloc. The country of Yugoslavia, officially founded in 1929, began dissolving in 1991. After much fighting and loss of life during the 1990s, the new map of what used to be Yugoslavia now shows seven different countries: Bosnia/Herzegovina, Croatia, Kosovo, Macedonia, Montenegro, Serbia, and Slovenia.

With all these border changes, ethnic groups sometimes became stranded in different countries. It is too simplistic to look at Hungary and think only of Hungarians, and Romania and think only of Romanians, for example. During the time of the Austro-Hungarian Empire, Hungary used to be much larger; its territory included part of Romania. When the war ended and Hungary lost part of its territory to Romania, millions of ethnic Hungarians remained behind, now citizens of a new country.

In much the same way, after the Soviet Union broke up into a number of smaller countries during the 1980s and 1990s, many ethnic groups remained where they had lived. In Ukraine about 17 percent of the population is Russian, and in Latvia and Estonia about 30 percent is Russian. About 5 percent of Uzbekistan's population is Tajik, and 25 percent of Tajikistan's population is Uzbek.

➤ OPPOSITE: An 1882 map of the northern portion of the Empire of Germany.

EMPIRE OF
GERMANY.
(NORTHERN PORTION)
The Kingdom of PRUSSIA is Coloured Red.

Scale of English Miles

Railways
Hohenzollern which belongs to Prussia shown on Map of Southern Portion.

Longitude East from Greenwich

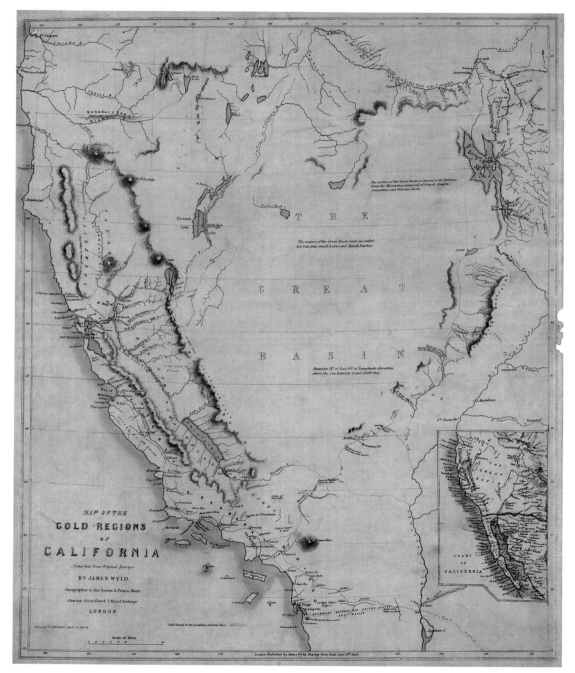

MAP OF THE
GOLD REGIONS
OF
CALIFORNIA

Compiled from Original Surveys

BY JAMES WYLD

Geographer to the Queen & Prince Albert

Charing Cross East & 2 Royal Exchange
LONDON

There's Gold in Them Hills!

NOTHING INSPIRES people to drop everything and chase their dreams quite like the promise of untold riches. This is exactly what happened after gold was discovered by James Marshall at Sutter's Mill in Coloma, California, in January 1848. Once word spread of his discovery, thousands of Americans headed to the West Coast to seek their glittering fortune. And these prospectors-to-be had to learn their geography to get to the gold fields.

Depending on where they were coming from, these fortune seekers made the journey either by the overland route or by sea, singing, "Ho, boys, ho! To California go! There's plenty of gold, so we are told, on the banks of the Sacramento!" If they chose the overland route, they had to find the best route to California from their location, encountering Native Americans, mountains, deserts, and great rivers along the way. If they chose the sea route, they would board a ship heading south to the Isthmus of Panama. When they arrived, they would cross the Isthmus to the Pacific side on foot and wait to be picked up by a ship headed for San Francisco. From San Francisco, they had to head up the San Pablo or the Suisan Bay to the Sacramento River, until they reached Sutter's Mill. From the famous mill, the prospectors would go across the valley to the foothills, where they could

➢ Map of the California gold district, 1849.

stake a claim. One California map, published in 1848, offered helpful details such as "gold found on this river" or "hills containing gold sub soil," while another outlined the gold-bearing rivers and creeks with yellow ink.

The craze in California was replayed elsewhere in the West: in Nevada with the discovery of silver deposits in the 1850s, in Colorado with the discovery of silver in the 1860s and 1870s, and in Alaska and British Columbia during the Klondike Gold Rush of the late 1890s. The huge flood of settlers made many places quickly grow from territory to statehood. California became a state in 1850, Nevada in 1864, and Colorado in 1876.

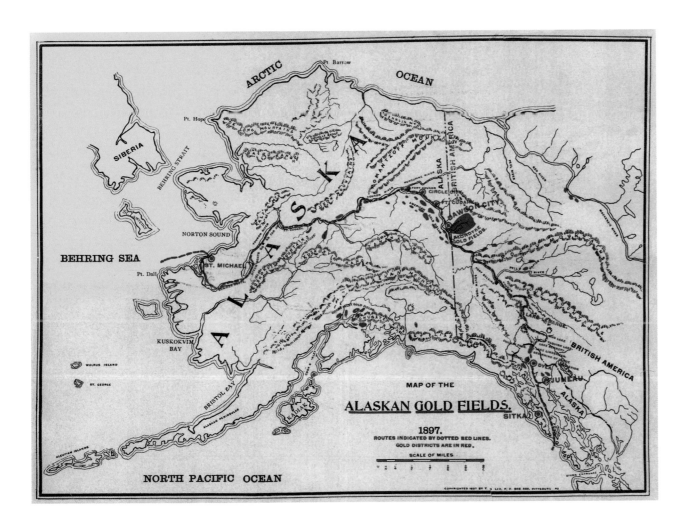

➤ Alaskan gold fields, 1897.

Treasure Maps

GOLD AND silver seekers surely used maps and a knowledge of geography to help them find the treasures they sought. But what about those seeking buried treasure? You probably have heard of the treasure map, that mysterious old document where an X marks the spot.

While pirates such as the legendary Captain Kidd sometimes did bury their treasure, there are no documented cases of an actual pirate treasure map. Fictional stories popularized the treasure map in the public imagination.

The author James Fenimore Cooper is perhaps best known for his book *The Last of the Mohicans*, but he was also the father of the treasure map. In his 1849 book *The Sea Lions*, two mysterious old charts are mentioned:

> *It was a solemn, as well as an anxious moment to the deacon, when he first raised the lid of the chest . . . he had no certainty that he should find even on the charts, the places of which he sought the latitudes and longitudes. . . . There were two old, dirty, and ragged charts, and on these the deacon laid his hands, much as the hawk, in its swoop, descends on its prey. As it did, however, a tremor came over him, that actually compelled him to throw himself into a chair, and to rest for a moment.*

> *The first of the charts opened, the deacon saw at a glance, was that of the Antarctic circle. There, sure enough, was laid down in ink, three or four specks for islands, with lat. — , —", and long. — , —", written out at its side. We are under obligations not to give the figures that stand on the chart, for the discovery is deemed to be important, by those who possess the secret, even to the present hour. . . .*

> *He wrote the latitude and longitude in a memorandum-book that he carried on his person; after which he again sat down, and with great care erased the island and the writing from the chart, with the point of a penknife. This done, his mind felt infinitely relieved. Nor was this all. Charts purchased for the schooner were lying on a table in his own room, and he projected on one of them, as well as his skill would allow, the sealing-islands he had just removed from the chart left by Daggett. There he also wrote, in pencil, the important figures that we are commanded not to reveal.*

However, it was not until later that the idea of the treasure map would really take hold of the American imagination. The adventure writer Robert Louis Stevenson was very interested in geography and maps. He wrote in 1895: "I have always been fond of maps, and can voyage in an atlas with the greatest enjoyment. The names of places are singularly inviting; the contour of coast and rivers is enthralling to the eye; and to hit, in a map, upon some place you have heard of before, makes history a new possession."

Stevenson's most famous book, *Treasure Island* (1883), was in fact born entirely from a map. The inspiration came in 1881 when the Stevenson family spent some time in a cottage in Scotland. The weather during their stay was miserable. It was especially unfortunate because Stevenson's young stepson, Lloyd Osbourne, was there and becoming bored. To entertain the child, Stevenson drew pictures. One day, he found himself drawing a treasure map straight from his own imagination, complete with names. He even colored the map to make it look more exciting.

Stevenson later wrote: "As I pored upon my map of Treasure Island the future characters of the book began to appear there visibly among imaginary woods; and their brown faces and bright weapons peeped out upon me from unexpected quarters, as they passed to and fro, fighting and hunting treasure, on these few square inches of a flat projection. The next thing I knew, I had some paper before me and was writing out a list of chapters."

Not only was Stevenson's story inspired by the treasure map, but the map also was a critical part of the plot. The popular book quickly became a classic, and it has since been published in many editions and languages. *Treasure Island* sparked the popular imagination and made "treasure

TREASURE SEARCH

THOUGH treasure maps are mostly a thing of fiction, that should not stop you from making your own and having your friends try to locate the loot.

YOU'LL NEED

➤ A treasure of your choosing (coins, trading cards, etc.—something you are willing to part with)
➤ Small cardboard jewelry box (or similar box)
➤ A backyard, school yard, or park
➤ Shovel
➤ Piece of white 8½-by-11-inch paper
➤ Pen
➤ Magnetic compass
➤ Friend

Place the treasure in the small box. Find a spot outside where you want to bury the treasure. The best place would be one where a disturbance (your digging and then filling a hole) will not look obvious. For example, an area where there is no grass growing, perhaps covered in old leaves, might work best. Use the shovel to dig a shallow hole, about six inches deep, and place the box inside. Fill the hole, making sure to smooth the surface with your shoe.

Now, find a "starting point" where you want your friend to begin searching for the treasure. Mark that on a piece of paper with a square. Create the map by taking steps in different directions and writing down the instructions until you reach the spot where you buried the treasure. For example, "Take 21 paces to the old oak tree, then 10 paces in the direction of the park bench. Go left for 18 paces and then go right for 14 paces. Take 24 paces in the direction of the schoolhouse, and there you should begin to dig." Mark your directions on the map using arrows and words. Mark the treasure with an X.

If you want to make the map more interesting, use a compass to tell your friend which directions to go. Once your friend finds the treasure, have him bury a treasure for you to find.

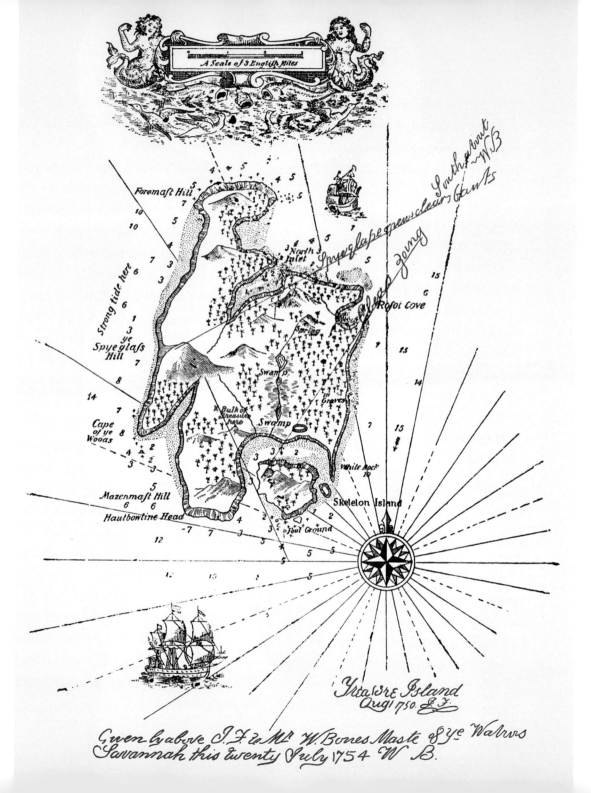

map" a commonly used term. During the 20th century and into the 21st, many books have been written and movies filmed about maps and charts showing clues to the location of vast riches.

However, beyond the obvious thrills of a treasure map, Robert Louis Stevenson believed that ordinary maps were essential tools for fiction writers of all types, not only for those writing adventure stories. To him, a map could not only make the details of a story more realistic but also provide inspiration.

The author must know his countryside, whether real or imaginary, like his hand; the distances, the points of the compass, the place of the sun's rising, the behavior of the moon, should all be beyond cavil.... With... the map of the country and the plan of every house, either actually plotted on paper or clearly and immediately apprehended in the mind, a man may hope to avoid some of the grossest possible blunders. With the map before him, he will scarce allow the sun to set in the east ... it is my contention— my superstition, if you like—that he who is faithful to his map, and consults it, and draws from it his inspiration, daily and hourly gains positive support, and not mere

➤ The original map from the book *Treasure Island* by Robert Louis Stevenson, published in 1883.

negative immunity from accident. The tale has a root there; it grows in that soil; it has a spine of its own behind the words. Better if the country be real, and he has walked every foot of it and knows every milestone. But, even with imaginary places, he will do well in the beginning to provide a map. As he studies it, relations will appear that he had not thought upon. He will discover obvious though unsuspected short cuts and footpaths for his messengers; and even when a map is not all the plot . . . it will be found to be a mine of suggestion.

Red States and Blue States

An understanding of geography is essential for anyone who wants to be a politician. A candidate must know her future constituents, or the people she will represent. Whether running for mayor, congressperson, senator, governor, or president, a political candidate has to know the differences between the regions he or she will represent. The higher the office sought, the more territory covered and the more geography comes into play.

A presidential candidate faces a difficult task— to learn as much as possible about all the different geographical areas of the country. While campaigning in Minnesota, the candidate is expected to know the unemployment statistics there, the

The Uncharted Desert Island

The world often seems like a very small place. Is it any wonder that our popular culture likes to imagine out-of-the-way places that don't appear on maps? *Gilligan's Island*, a television sitcom that originally ran from 1964 to 1967, featured a cast of seven people whose tour boat went off course from Hawaii, leaving them stranded on an uncharted, deserted island somewhere in the Pacific. More recently, the television series *Lost* imagined people stranded on a mysterious island after an airplane crash.

The idea of the "uncharted isle" is a romantic notion that has appeared many times in popular culture. In the book *Robinson Crusoe* by Daniel Defoe, published in 1719, a man is stranded on a remote island off the coast of South America. Toward the beginning, the narrator writes:

➤ Robinson Crusoe on his island.

> *Where I was, I yet knew not; whether on the continent or an island . . . there was a hill not above a mile from me which rose up very steep and high. . . . I travelled for discovery up to the top of that hill. . . . I saw my fate . . . that I was in an island environed on every side by the sea: no land to be seen except some rocks, which lay a great way off; and two small islands less than this, which lay about three league to the west.*

In *Swiss Family Robinson* by Johann David Wyss, published in 1812, four boys get stranded with their parents on a deserted island. And in 2000, Tom Hanks starred in the movie *Cast Away*, about a man stranded on an uncharted island for four years after his plane crashed in the ocean.

major cities, the customs, and the special needs of Minnesotans.

Because of the way our Constitution is set up, the president is elected not by an overall popular vote but on a state-by-state basis. The winner of the popular vote in each state gets all of its electoral votes. The number of electoral votes is equal to the number of US senators (always two) plus the number of US representatives (directly proportional to the state's population). So, as a presidential election approaches, the nation becomes fascinated by a special kind of map: the electoral map.

Presidential campaign strategies are heavily based upon the mathematics of how to get to the required 270 electoral votes. Strategists study the electoral map to understand what combinations of states would help candidates win. Candidates campaign more often in states where the polls show the people are undecided about whom to vote for, and less often in states that are already colored red (to represent likely Republican victories) or blue (to represent probable Democratic wins) on the electoral map.

Modern technology allows anyone to go online and play a strategist, coloring the states red or blue to see how the numbers could add up to victory for one side or the other. On election night, the entire country (and the world) watches the news as the states are colored in over the course of the night. Political reporters, commentators, and analysts can then look at these maps and discuss why people in certain area voted the way they did, and how that compares to the way those areas voted in previous elections.

With the latest mapping technology, television news analysts can stand in front of a screen and zoom in on a particular state to show the concentration of red and blue at the greatest level of detail that the data will allow.

However, electoral maps are deceptive because their "look" doesn't reflect the reality of the vote.

➤ This mechanical "Presidential Muddle Puzzle" (1894) mimicked the electoral system and allowed people to solve logic challenges, state by state.

Presidential victories are often won through the smaller, more densely populated states. For example, the huge state of Montana has three electoral votes, while tiny Massachusetts has 12. Big red Montana looks like a greater victory than tiny blue Massachusetts, but it isn't; Massachusetts offers four times as many electoral votes.

➤ The electoral map as of November 7, 2008, when there was still an "undecided" state.

UNITED STATES PRESIDENTIAL ELECTION 2008
RESULTS BY STATE
November 7, 2008

Geography and Maps Present and Future

ALL MAPS are views of what the world looks like from above, so it makes sense that we should use actual aerial photos to create more accurate maps. But for thousands of years, outside of climbing a hill or mountain, humans have been unable to get an aerial view. The so-called bird's-eye views were not taken from the air; they were only an artist's idea of what an aerial view would look like.

The first true aerial photographs were taken from a hot-air balloon in the 19th century. As the 20th century progressed and then turned to the 21st, new technology allowed us reach higher into the sky, up into space, and create more precise maps of earth, as well as the other planets in our solar system.

Aerial Photography

THE HOT-AIR balloon was the first invention that allowed people to take flight into the sky. The first manned flight of a balloon was in France in 1783, when Jean-François Pilâtre de Rozier (1754–85) was able to stay in the air for 25 minutes.

Balloon flight soon became popular, allowing balloonists to clearly see and appreciate the topog-raphy of the land below. Still, there was really no practical way to do a meaningful survey from above. With the invention and improvement of the camera, it became possible to take photographs from the air. The first aerial photograph was taken from a balloon floating 250 feet over French soil in 1858 by Felix Nadar (1820–1910), a French pho-tographer who became famous for constructing his own balloons and taking aerial photographs.

➢ ABOVE: An 1867 cartoon of Felix Nadar, French balloon photographer.

➢ RIGHT: A photograph of Manhattan, New York, taken from a balloon in 1906.

Balloon photography continued to develop and improve during the remainder of the 19th century. Balloons were briefly used for reconnaissance during the US Civil War.

Beginning in 1882, a new method of aerial photography was devised: sending a camera aloft through the use of kites. A man named George Lawrence used 17 kites to take photographs of San Francisco after the earthquake and fire of 1906. Though this method was innovative, it was not practical for regular use.

Aerial views would experience a rebirth with the invention of the airplane in the early 20th century, so that by the time of World War I, aerial photography was widely used. Images taken from the air were used to create military maps for use in war strategy.

Because airplanes move at great speeds and experience air turbulence, improvements in camera technology made a great difference in the quality and usefulness of aerial photographs. The Fairchild Aerial Camera Corporation was a pioneer in taking aerial photographs on a large scale.

When carefully taken, aerial photographs can be used to create base maps, to which more details can later be added. The science of converting aerial images to maps is called *photogrammetry*. Because an airplane's camera can be directly above only one point when a photograph is taken, there will be more distortion in the photograph

AERONAUTICAL CHARTS

In the 1920s and early 1930s, when visual navigation was still common, the US Coast and Geodetic Survey produced airway strip maps. These narrow charts were designed to help pilots fly popular routes. Each map noted the various airfields, beacons, railroad tracks, highways, and other visual landmarks.

Before long, the government realized that the strip maps were not enough, and sectional charts were printed, covering entire areas. Between 1935 and 1946, 28 Regional Aeronautical Charts were published by USC&GS (11 of them covered Alaska, the rest the contiguous United States). Other maps for pilots included instrument approach and landing charts and radio facility (RF) charts. The first RF charts were published in 1942 and were designed to aid in instrument navigation.

During World War II, 120 charts of the Western Hemisphere were produced to help in the war effort. Aeronautical charts are still widely used today, especially by civilian and military pilots.

➤ This 1929 aeronautical strip chart shows the route between St. Louis and Chicago.

> Marine gliders in the sky near Parris Island, South Carolina, in 1942. Anyone who has ever flown in an airplane can appreciate the value of aerial views to understanding geography.

farther away from that point. This type of photo is fine for purely visual purposes, but not to create a map. To fix this distortion, overlapping photos have to be used to create a "stereo" image that is more accurate.

At first, the features of aerial photographs were traced by hand to create maps. More recently, aerial or satellite photographs have been converted into digital images using something called an analytical photogrammetric stereoplotter. The stereoplotters can automatically correct things such as the curvature of the earth, variations in aircraft altitude, and variations in ground elevation.

Aerial photographs are useful to many scientists and historians, who can use them to study everything from ecology to property lines. Archaeologists use aerial photographs because they can reveal patterns in the growth of grass and vegetation. Changes in the color and fullness of vegetation can mean there are features, such as walls, buried under the surface. Infrared aerial photographs are helpful in revealing ruins located deep within jungles.

The federal government has used aerial photographs to help with mapping and other projects. Some of the earliest aerial photography was for the Department of Agriculture, beginning in the 1930s. A program called the National High Altitude Photography (NHAP) program ran from 1980 to 1989; its goal was to create complete aerial coverage of the lower 48 states. Planes took photographs from 40,000 feet with two cameras, one containing black-and-white film and the other, color infrared. The NHAP black-and-white photographs cover 129 square miles, and the longer NHAP color-infrared photographs cover 68 square miles.

In 1987, a new program was introduced. The National Aerial Photography Program (NAPP) was created for mapping, resource planning, engineering, land use planning, and agricultural monitoring. For this program, images are snapped from aircraft flying at an altitude of 20,000 feet, and they cover 32 square miles.

Imaging the Earth from Space: The Landsat Story

As HUMANS began to send rockets and probes into space during the 1950s and 1960s, scientists realized the great potential of photographing the earth from space. If properly equipped, satellites in orbit around the earth could provide a much more uniform and complete picture of the earth's surface than airplanes could. In 1966, the director of the US Geological Survey (USGS) had the idea to create a special program to launch satellites for the specific purpose of studying the earth.

After a few years of discussion and testing, by 1970 NASA had the authorization and funding to build a remote sensing satellite. On July 23, 1972, Landsat 1—then known as the Earth Resources Technology Satellite, or ERTS—was launched. Though photographs had been taken from space before, Landsat 1 marked the first time a satellite was launched with a main purpose of studying the surface of the earth.

Landsat 1 was equipped with a camera system called the Return Beam Vidicon (RBV), and a Multispectral Scanner System (MSS). Malfunctions of the RBV caused the MSS, which used a

➤ Pre-Columbian ruins were revealed in the rain forests of Costa Rica during NASA's AirSAR 2004 Mesoamerica campaign. AirSAR (Airborne Synthetic Aperture Radar) has high-resolution sensors that allow it to penetrate clouds and see beneath treetops. *Courtesy of NASA*

➤ Artist's rendering of Landsat 7 in orbit above the earth. *Courtesy of NASA*

ated until January 1978, far outliving its projected useful life. In the five and a half years that it photographed, Landsat 1 sent back more than 300,000 images of the earth.

The United States has launched additional earth-imaging satellites since then, the most recent of which was Landsat 7 in 1999. India, France, the Soviet Union, China/Brazil (jointly), Germany/Russia (jointly), and Japan have also launched similar imaging satellites over the years. Images of the earth shot from space continue to provide scientists with rich cartographic and ecological information about our entire planet, and provide insight into the shrinking of the Amazon rain forests and global warming, among other things. It is especially useful having data going back to 1972; this allows scientists to study the many changes in the planet and make predictions for the future. By comparing early images with more recent images, for example, scientists have studied the sedimentation (filling in with soil and sand) of the Mississippi Delta and deforestation (cutting down of trees) in Bolivia.

The detailed images of the earth from the Landsat satellites were used to study many things, including water resources and ecology, retreating glaciers, the aftereffects of the eruption of the Mount St. Helens volcano in Washington state in 1980, the aftermath of Hurricane Katrina in 2005 (the images from Landsat helped scientists estimate flood water depth and coverage in New

special mirror, to become the primary on-board recording system. A team of 300 scientists helped to interpret the data that the satellite sent back to earth in green, red, and two infrared (heat detecting) bands. Each band emphasized different features: water, land, vegetation, buildings, and more.

Landsat 1 orbited the earth at an altitude of 920 kilometers and circled the earth every 103 minutes, making 14 orbits per day. The satellite oper-

Orleans), as well as the effects of wildfires, floods, avalanches, earthquakes, and many other natural disasters. These images not only provide information about the disasters themselves but also assist in planning for recovery efforts.

In 2008, the USGS opened its full Landsat archive to the general public. As of 2011, Landsat 5 and Landsat 7 were still in operation. Landsat 7 orbits the earth once every 99 minutes at an altitude of 438 miles (705 km) and captures about 300 scenes per day. Landsat imagery is used by programs such as Google Earth, which allow the user to zoom in on any part of the globe and see high-resolution satellite imagery, down to houses, cars, and sometimes even people.

Geographic Information Systems (GIS)

ACCORDING TO the USGS, GIS is "a computer system capable of capturing, storing, analyzing, and displaying geographically referenced information; that is, data identified according to location." In other words, GIS is the capture and use of digital data to be applied to maps in multiple layers and analyzed. GIS data can include roads, census data, topography, rivers, geological data, soils, land use, and many other types of data, which can all be placed onto a base map individually or layered in combination with each other.

➤ Landsat 7 image of Gosses Bluff, Australia, 2002. *Courtesy of USGS*

Introduced during the 1960s, the Canada Geographic Information System (CGIS) was one of the first GIS systems. It was designed specifically to help the government examine land data for agricultural use, such as developing land use plans for large rural parts of the country. In 1969, the Environmental Systems Research Institute (ESRI) was founded, which would later produce software called ArcInfo, a widely used GIS application.

The possible uses of GIS are almost limitless. For example, biologists placed collar transmitters on caribou and polar bears to track their migration routes for a 21-month period. This layer of geographic information could then be laid over maps showing the locations of planned oil drilling sites. In this way, the researchers could figure out whether the animals' migration routes would be disturbed by any of the development plans.

GIS can even be used to create three-dimensional maps and animations. The US Forest Service used three-dimensional maps of Arizona's Prescott National Forest to determine the effects that mining would have on the area.

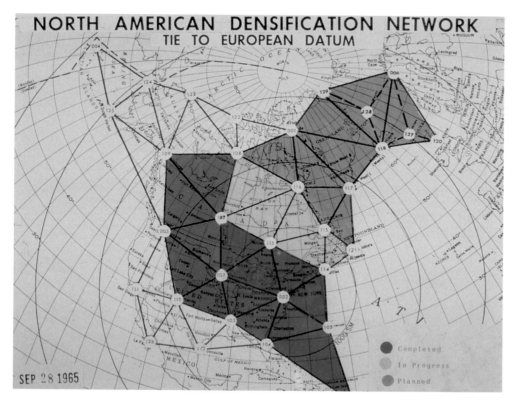

Global Positioning System (GPS)

ANOTHER RECENT innovation is the Global Positioning System (GPS), a US Air Force–run navigation system that is free to anyone with a GPS receiver. It became operational in 1981. Using data received from 24 satellites orbiting the earth, the Global Navigation Satellite System (GNSS) provides GPS receivers with latitude, longitude, and altitude year-round, 24 hours a day, in any kind of weather.

GPS is often used in combination with GIS to provide detailed information on one's location. In fact, GPS can also be used to plot the location of landmarks, and that information can then be fed into a GIS for future use. GPS has many applications, including "precision agriculture," which allows farmers to pinpoint soil conditions and irrigation-related improvements, among other things. If farmers know exactly what sections of their land are driest or have the poorest soil, they can adjust their irrigation and fertilization to match it.

Mapping is much easier with GPS. One surveyor with GPS can accomplish as much in a single day as a team of surveyors without GPS could accomplish in weeks. Drivers of cars equipped

➤ This 1965 image illustrates the North American Densification Network, a program to provide geographic information using satellite triangulation (the ability to determine a location based on its distance from three or more satellites). This program, since abandoned, was an ancestor of the GPS currently in operation. *Courtesy of NOAA*

with a GPS transmitter always know their location, making getting lost a thing of the past.

Mapping Software

For about 90 years, taking a family automobile trip, whether 30 miles to a nearby town or 3,000 miles across the country, involved the same preparations: finding the road map, studying the best possible route, and navigating along the way. During the trip, a chorus of, "Are we there yet?" would ring out from the back seat, and parents would glance at the map and say a firm "Not yet."

These days, you can type two street addresses anywhere in the country into a mapping program and get a set of precise door-to-door directions. These directions are based upon stored details of the entire country's road and street address systems. They tell you how many miles to travel on what road, where to turn, and about how long the ride will take. The program selects the "best" route from all the possible ones. It can also generate a close-up street map of any neighborhood in the country. Satellite imagery feeding into the program allows you to switch between map view and satellite view, so you can see trees, rivers, and mountains from above.

Letting a computer program decide your route makes travel easy and asking for directions unnecessary. However, sometimes what the program says is the shortest route is actually not, and sometimes the shortest route is not the fastest route. Map reading still requires the human touch; even the most sophisticated mapping programs cannot tell you if roads are bumpy, under construction, flooded, or accident-plagued.

SATELLITE PHOTO TO STREET MAP

MANY modern maps are created from aerial or satellite photos. In this activity, you can try your hand at translating an aerial view to a map.

You'll Need
➤ Access to a computer and mapping program
➤ Printer
➤ Tracing paper
➤ Pencil

Find your neighborhood using a mapping program on the Internet. Two good examples are Google Earth and MapQuest. These programs may have both satellite view and street view available, depending on your location.

Print out a satellite view of your neighborhood and try to trace the streets. What do you think is the best time of year for taking aerial photos that can be accurately converted to street maps? Look carefully at the images of your street and your neighborhood. What clues can you look for to help you determine how recent the images are? For example, are there new buildings in your neighborhood? Have old ones been torn down? Did neighbors put an addition on their house? Perhaps a tree was planted or fell down in a storm.

Space Geography: Mapping the Planets

HUMANS HAVE been looking to the skies for thousands of years. The ancient Greeks were the first to make star maps, connecting the stars to form pictures, called constellations. As soon as Galileo invented the telescope in the early 17th century, astronomers were able to study the surface of the moon and map its features.

However, even the best telescope can give only limited information about the moon and our neighboring planets. It was not until the age of space exploration that scientists were able to begin to study the moon, Mars, Venus, and Mercury up close.

The earliest spacecraft were not able to take photographs. *Mars 1* was the first spacecraft to fly by Mars, in 1962, but it provided only limited data before losing contact with mission controllers. *Mariner 2* flew by Venus in 1962, also gathering limited data.

With later missions, improved technology allowed for better observation. *Mariner 4* flew by Mars in 1964 but returned only 22 images. *Mariner 6* was able to take 49 long-range and 26 close-range images in 1969. These pictures showed heavily cratered areas on Mars that resembled parts of the moon. *Mariner 7* also flew by the planet in 1969, taking 93 long-range and 33 close-range images. The photos the spacecraft sent back to earth gave us some ideas of what Mars's surface was like.

The first moon landing in 1969, and later manned missions, gave us an excellent look at the features of our planet's only satellite.

When *Mariner 9* reached Mars in 1971, it orbited the red planet for a year, recording many details about the cratered surface of the planet's southern half and the volcanoes of the northern half. *Mariner 10*, launched in 1973, made three flybys of Mercury and photographed half the planet's moonlike surface. The biggest Mars development came in 1976, when *Viking 1* actually landed on the surface. An orbiter also conducted infrared thermal mapping from above.

➤ Map of the moon's surface hand-colored at the Kennedy Space Center a few days before the November 1969 *Apollo 12* mission to the moon. The map was requested by the *Apollo 12* crew.
Courtesy of USGS

Launched in 1978, *Pioneer Venus 1* orbited that planet for 14 years and used radar to map the surface in detail, revealing a mountain 35,000 feet high, taller than Mount Everest. The data *Pioneer Venus 1* sent back to earth allowed scientists to create a topographic map of Venus's surface between 73 degrees north and 63 degrees south latitude, but the resolution was not very clear. *Magellan*, launched in 1989, was designed to map at least 70 percent of Venus's surface but succeeded in mapping 98 percent of it at a high resolution. These maps revealed that 85 percent of Venus is covered with volcanic flows.

The most recent planetary missions have been the most exciting. Launched in 2004, the *Messenger* spacecraft was only the second space mission to Mercury. *Messenger* is mapping nearly the entire planet in color, including most of the areas unseen by *Mariner 10*, and measuring the composition of the surface, atmosphere, and magnetosphere. Recent unmanned missions to Mars have included *Pathfinder, Spirit,* and *Opportunity,* roving vehicles that have landed on Mars and are providing new and exciting information about the geography of that planet.

The Future of Maps

MAPS WILL always be an important tool to help us get where we are going, whether it be from

MOON OBSERVATION

SINCE ancient times, people have studied the moon, but it was not until Galileo Galilei invented the telescope that we were able to magnify its surface. Galileo used two eyeglass lenses, one with a concave (curved inward) side and the other with a convex (curved outward) side. He put one lens at each end of a long metal tube. When he looked through the concave side, he was able to see that the objects he viewed were magnified several times. Once word began to spread of his invention, crowds of people visited Galileo and asked to look through the telescope. Galileo used the telescope to make important observations about the moon, including the height of the moon's mountains. In this activity, you'll view the moon using binoculars.

YOU'LL NEED
➤ Friend
➤ Binoculars
➤ Pad of white paper, 8½ by 11 Inches
➤ Pencil
➤ Digital camera
➤ Computer
➤ Printer
➤ Tracing paper

Most modern binoculars are as powerful as the telescope Galileo invented. On a night when the moon is full or nearly full, have a friend hold your binoculars in place so you can observe the moon (or have your friend hold the pad of paper for you while you hold the binoculars with one hand and draw with the other). Use a pencil to draw your view of the moon through the binoculars.

Next, try using a digital camera to zoom in on the moon. Snap a few pictures and upload them to your computer. Depending on the quality of your camera, you may be able to enlarge the pictures on your computer before printing them out. Place a sheet of tracing paper over the best photo printout, and trace the craters and other features you notice. (You don't need to go back out another night to capture a different side of the moon; the same side of the moon always faces earth.)

Find where the moon landings took place by researching online. Estimate the sites of the landings on your moon map and mark them, along with their dates. This website has a great illustration of the landings, both manned and unmanned: www.time.com /time/2008/moon_landings/.

> Above: This enhanced-color, 360-degree "Gallery Panorama" of the *Pathfinder* landing site on Mars was obtained in July 1997. The *Sojourner* rover is shown next to the large rock nicknamed "Yogi." *Courtesy of USGS*

one town to another or from one solar system to another. And they will always be useful in helping us study ourselves.

As technology improves, the possibilities for mapping are endless. The federal government has already taken a step toward the future with www .nationalatlas.gov, a comprehensive website that has a wide variety of maps of the United States available at the click of a mouse, including customized maps to suit anyone's interests. The future of maps is exciting because the average person will have access to all kinds of highly advanced, specialized maps.

The web has helped make maps even more fun, using different tools such as animation. For example, you can now easily see the spread of invasive zebra mussels in our waterways through an animated series of maps.

Another amazing example of modern web-based map technology is a series of monthly maps showing vegetation cover of the United States. The government uses Advanced Very High Resolution Radiometer (AVHRR) images collected by Television Infrared Observation Satellites. The data from these satellites is used to calculate a vegetation index representing the quantity of vegetation

and the amount of photosynthesis activity.

With better and more detailed maps of our natural resources, scientists will be able to develop solutions to help us save and protect our planet.

And, as we continue to explore space, we will be able to map the planets in even greater detail, preparing for a possible manned mission to Mars and beyond.

➤ RIGHT: Landsat images from 1975, 1992, and 2000 show the deforestation in Bolivia over time. *Courtesy of USGS*

GLOSSARY

Antarctic Circle: Line of latitude that runs parallel to the equator and 66 degrees and 33 minutes south of it, marking the edge of the frigid zone surrounding the South Pole.

Arctic Circle: Line of latitude that runs parallel to the equator and 66 degrees and 33 minutes north of it, marking the edge of the frigid zone surrounding the North Pole.

axis: Imaginary line passing north-south through the center of the earth, around which the earth spins on a daily basis.

bird's-eye view: A three-dimensional look at a town or city as if seen from the point of view of a bird hundreds or thousands of feet in the sky flying toward the settlement.

cartography: The science of mapmaking.

compass north: The direction in which a compass points, usually several degrees off from true north due to variations in the magnetic fields of the earth. Also known as magnetic north.

contour lines: Lines on a topographic map that mark all the points at a certain altitude, usually in increments of anywhere from 10 feet to 100 feet or more. Contour lines give the map's user an idea of how steep or gentle the slopes of a mountain or hill are.

cultural geography: The study of human-related features as they relate to place, including a location's people, cities, languages, etc. *See also* physical geography.

equator: Imaginary line at 0 degrees latitude, running east-west around the earth halfway between the North and South Poles and dividing the earth into the Northern and Southern Hemispheres.

fault: The boundary where two of the earth's plates meet; often the location of volcanic or earthquake activity.

geodimeter: An instrument that measures the distance between two points.

geography: The study of place and all things related to it, including both physical (natural) and cultural (human-related) features.

glaciation: The covering of parts of the earth by advancing ice sheets during one of several ice ages that our planet has experienced.

gnomonic projection: The oldest map projection, said to have been created by Thales, a sixth-century-B.C. Greek mathematician.

hemisphere: From the Greek meaning "half-sphere," this usually refers to the northern and southern halves of the earth (divided at the equator), but it can also refer to the western and eastern halves (divided at the prime meridian).

landforms: The natural features of a location—mountains, hills, plains, deserts, canyons, streams, rivers, lakes, oceans, peninsulas, and islands.

latitude: Imaginary lines running east-west around the earth, indicating the distance from the equator. That distance is expressed in degrees; there are 360 degrees of latitude, 180 in the Northern Hemisphere and 180 in the Southern Hemisphere.

lithography: A method for printing maps that involves drawing map details in reverse on a special stone treated with chemicals to attract and repel ink.

longitude: Imaginary lines running north-south around the earth, indicating the distance from the prime meridian. That distance is expressed in degrees; there are 360 degrees of longitude, 180 in the Eastern Hemisphere and 180 in the Western Hemisphere.

magnetic declination: The difference between true north and compass (magnetic) north. It fluctuates from year to year, and varies depending on one's location.

magnetic north: *See* compass north.

map projection: A technique for depicting the three-dimensional surface of the earth in two dimensions, such as on a flat paper map. *See also* Mercator projection, gnomonic projection.

marine chronometer: A precise clock that keeps perfect time at sea, allowing sailors to determine longitude.

Mercator projection: A map projection devised by Gerardus Mercator that imagines that the earth sphere is placed into an upright cylinder, points on the sphere are projected onto the cylinder's wall, and the cylinder is then rolled out flat. For centuries, the Mercator projection was one of the most popular projections used by cartographers.

meridian: One of 37 different north-south reference lines used in the Public Land Survey System. The term is also used to refer to lines of longitude.

metes and bounds system: Method of surveying that describes pieces of land using natural landmarks (such as trees, rocks, and rivers) and man-made landmarks (such as buildings) as base points.

nautical charts: Maps showing coastal areas or open waters. They include information such as water depth and the direction of currents, and show islands, sandbars, lighthouses, and other pertinent landmarks.

Pangaea: Name given to the massive supercontinent that was supposedly created hundreds of millions of years ago when the continents drifted together.

parallel: Another name for a line of latitude.

photo-auto map: An early-20th-century road map that featured detailed driving directions along with photographs of key landmarks along the way.

photogrammetry: The science of converting aerial photographs into maps, compensating for the distortion in the original images.

physical geography: Study of the physical (natural) features of a location. *See also* cultural geography.

plate tectonics: Widely accepted theory that says volcanic and earthquake activity is caused by the shifting of the earth's plates.

plates: The dozen major pieces into which the earth's crust is broken.

pole: Point located at either end (north or south) of the earth's axis.

prime meridian: Imaginary line at 0 degrees longitude, running between the North and South poles and through Greenwich, England, dividing the earth into the Eastern and Western Hemispheres. Locating 0 degrees longitude was an arbitrary decision (unlike latitude, for which 0 was set at the equator, halfway between the North and South Poles), but an international conference agreed that the prime meridian would pass through Greenwich.

right-of-way: Strips of land along the either side of railroad tracks given by the government to the railroad companies.

scale: A set ratio of map distance to actual distance. For example, a scale of 1:5,000 would mean that 1 map inch equals 5,000 inches.

surveyor: Someone who uses tools to determine the exact boundaries of a property or to chart physical details such as altitude or the location of natural features such as rivers.

topographic map: Map showing physical features, especially elevations.

topography: The details of the earth's surface features.

Tropic of Cancer: Line of latitude that runs parallel to the equator and 23½ degrees north of it, marking the northern edge of the earth's tropical region.

Tropic of Capricorn: Line of latitude that runs parallel to the equator and 23½ degrees south of it, marking the southern edge of the earth's tropical region.

true north: The direction of the actual North Pole, at the top of the earth sphere. *See also* compass north.

upper mantle: The molten layer below the earth's crust.

SELECTED BIBLIOGRAPHY

Alexander, Heather. *A Child's Introduction to the World: Geography, Cultures, and People—from the Grand Canyon to the Great Wall of China*. Illustrated by Meredith Hamilton. New York: Black Dog & Leventhal, 2010.

Arnold, Caroline. *The Geography Book: Activities for Exploring, Mapping, and Enjoying Your World*. New York: Wiley, 2002.

DK Publishing. *Geography of the World*. New York: DK Publishing, 2006.

Gardner, Jane P., and J. Elizabeth Mills. *The Everything Kids' Geography Book: From the Grand Canyon to the Great Barrier Reef—Explore the World!* Avon, MA: Adams Media, 2009.

Sutcliffe, Andrea. *The New York Public Library Amazing US Geography: A Book of Answers for Kids*. New York: Wiley, 2001

Veregin, Howard, ed. *Goode's World Atlas*. 22nd ed. Chicago: Rand McNally, 2009.

ONLINE RESOURCES TO EXPLORE

Library of Congress Map Collections

http://memory.loc.gov/ammem/browse/ListSome
.php?category=Maps

An excellent assortment of maps of practically every country in the world.

National Atlas

www.nationalatlas.gov/index.html

An interactive site that allows you to build your own map of the United States based on a wide variety of data.

NOAA Photo Gallery

www.photolib.noaa.gov

Images pertaining to the seas, and to exploration and surveying in general.

NASA Image Galleries

www.nasa.gov/multimedia/imagegallery/

Images pertaining to space exploration.

US Geological Survey Multimedia Gallery

http://gallery.usgs.gov/

Images from the USGS collection pertaining to the geology and topography of the earth, including Landsat images.

INDEX

Page numbers in **bold** indicate maps or photographs.